OVER FLOW

Also by Tom Berlin and Lovett H. Weems Jr.
Bearing Fruit: Ministry with Real Results

To subscribe to the Lewis Center for Church Leadership's
free online newsletter, *Leading Ideas,* go to
www.churchleadership.com.

LOVETT H. WEEMS JR.
TOM BERLIN
OVER
FLOW

INCREASE WORSHIP ATTENDANCE
& BEAR MORE FRUIT

Abingdon Press™

Nashville

OVERFLOW
INCREASE WORSHIP ATTENDANCE & BEAR MORE FRUIT

This book is printed on acid-free paper.

Library of Congress Cataloging-in-Publication Data

Berlin, Tom.
Overflow : increase worship attendance and bear more fruit / by Tom Berlin and Lovett H. Weems, Jr.
pages   cm
Includes bibliographical references and index.
ISBN 978-1-4267-6751-7 (pbk., trade, adhesive, perfect binding : alk. paper)   1.   Church attendance.   2. Church growth.   3. Public worship.   I. Title.
BV652.5.B47 2013
254'.5—dc23

2013024420

All scripture quotations unless noted otherwise are taken from the Holy Bible, TODAY'S NEW INTERNATIONAL VERSION®. Copyright © 2001, 2005 International Bible Society. All rights reserved throughout the world. Used by permission of the International Bible Society.

Scripture marked (NRSV) is from the *New Revised Standard Version of the Bible*, copyright 1989, Division of Christian Education of the National Council of the Churches of Christ in the United States of America. Used by permission. All rights reserved.

Pages 9-11, "Visitor Feedback Survey," may be reproduced for the local congregation with the following credit line: From *Overflow: Increase Worship Attendance & Bear More Fruit* by Lovett H. Weems, Jr. and Tom Berlin. Copyright © 2013 by Abingdon Press. Copyright © 2013 by Lewis Center for Church Leadership, Wesley Theological Seminary. www.churchleadership.com.

15 16 17 18 19 20 21 22—10 9 8 7 6 5 4 3 2
MANUFACTURED IN THE UNITED STATES OF AMERICA

To

My parents, J. D. and Nancy Berlin,

*who placed worship at the center of our week
so that Christ would be at the center of our lives.*

T. B.

To

*The staff of the Lewis Center for Church Leadership
of Wesley Theological Seminary*

*with much appreciation for their commitment
to helping congregations
increase their capacity for service, vitality, and growth.*

L. H. W

CONTENTS

INTRODUCTION

All churches seek to experience the promise of Jesus that those "who abide in me and I in them bear much fruit" (John 15:5, NRSV). In *Bearing Fruit: Ministry with Real Results*, we illustrated how focusing on results or fruits of ministry shapes how we carry out ministry. We provided a procedure to ensure you are clear about the fruit that God is calling a ministry to produce. The key to this practice is two words: *so that*. The task is to complete this sentence: "We will do x *so that* y happens."[1]

Nowhere is the challenge of fruitfulness more important than in helping increasing numbers of people experience God through worship. It is the challenge of worship attendance to which we seek in this book to apply the lessons of fruitfulness. As we encourage others to do, we developed a "so that" statement for this book.

We have written this book

so that

congregational leaders learn strategic clues regarding worship attendance
that they can tailor to their situations and implement,
resulting in more people becoming and growing as Christian disciples
through increased participation in vital and life-changing worship.

Church leaders want to increase worship attendance and do make many efforts toward this goal. However, the reality in many churches is decline every year in worship attendance. This book seeks to give people hope that they can improve their attendance by not only offering to you encouragement about how important the task is, but also proposing practical steps to develop ways of planning, implementing, and evaluating worship that can produce greater fruitfulness. While examples from actual churches are central to the book, it is not a collection of random tips. There is a concept or theory to which the examples are attached so that readers can see these as simply examples of the insight, and they then can develop the expression of the insight most appropriate for their situation.

This book features a number of what the Lewis Center for Church Leadership calls "actionable strategic insights." The Lewis Center, where Lovett serves as director, defines these as practical steps people can take to act on a goal they have, without having to do major research. Insights and practices have emerged from applied research, which have been implemented by practitioners to great benefit. Another way to frame what we offer here is giving readers some new lenses through which to view the subject of worship attendance. Our readers are assumed to be those who care deeply about worship attendance and have a passion for more people gathering to worship God and, thus, becoming and growing as Christian disciples. Our goal is to give such motivated people tools they need to accomplish their goals.

WHY FOCUS ON WORSHIP ATTENDANCE?

Our goal is to assist you in doing what your church was established to do—help more people gather to worship God and leave inspired to serve others. At the heart of why any church exists is to glorify God and to share God as revealed in Jesus Christ; thus, worship is at the center of the congregation's life. The chances that God will speak to someone through your church are far greater if that person is in worship. Careful attention to the people you are seeking to reach, to planning, and to patterns of attendance can bear much fruit for God. The church, of course, is more than worship, but without vital worship attendance, it is unlikely that members are growing and new disciples are being brought to faith. Worship attendance is also the one factor where improvement tends to help every other aspect of the church's ministry.

Growing churches connect people with God, and compelling and inspiring worship is a primary means of connection. But there is not one right way to worship. When we look at growing churches, sometimes we think that if we simply copy their worship practices, we will grow also. We can certainly learn from every church that is reaching people for Christ, but no one way of worshiping is right for all churches. What is right for your church depends on a number of factors.

For example, some think that successful new church starts feature a certain worship style. This is not the case. Growing new churches do a good job of developing worship that connects with the needs of those they are seeking to reach. While the worship is different at various new church starts, the worship tends to be relevant to their particular contexts. This does not mean just doing what you have always done because it is comfortable for those attending. It means doing what fits your church's mission and its surrounding context today. If those who worship at your church are more representative of the community in a past era than today, perhaps your worship has not adapted to the needs of today. Current worshipers are indeed part of that context, but so are those whom you have not yet reached.

WHY NOW?

There is another reason for focusing on worship attendance. In recent years, it has become more difficult for churches to increase their worship attendance. After relatively strong attendance in the 1990s and a rise in attendance for five Sundays after the tragedy of September 11, 2001, attendance has been more likely to decrease instead of increase for most US churches since 2002.[2]

COMPONENTS OF FRUITFULNESS

We know that fruitfulness is one of many agricultural biblical images. It is good to remember how many things are required for a fruitful harvest. Rather than resist what may seem to be cumbersome details and processes, perhaps we should learn from the myriad components farmers require for fruitfulness. Ask any farmer of any crop whether it is possible to produce an abundant harvest from overgrown land, with out-of-date seeds, with unmotivated workers, or with ineffective tools, and you will get a look of unbelief that anyone would ask such a ridiculous question. Farmers have known for centuries the necessary components of a good crop year and the variables that will either enhance or hurt the harvest. Even though the exact shape of the final harvest is always out of the farmers' power to control, they still know they must have systems, processes, and standards to be responsible farmers.

One important concept from the world of agriculture is the distinction between capacity and yield.[3] Think of a farmer with so many acres of land. There are things the farmer can do to increase the yield on that land. Fertilizer, choice of seeds, irrigation, and harvesting equipment are just a few factors that might bring about a greater yield. But eventually there is a limit to growth by yield only. The farmer can focus, however, not just on yield but also on capacity. Buying or renting more land would be an example of a way of increasing capacity. To increase worship attendance, you will need to focus on some factors that have the potential of increasing capacity (reaching more people) and also on things that have the potential to increase yield (greater level of participation from current members).

It may seem strange to speak of these opportunities for churches when there are so many discouraging trends for many churches. Circumstances are not particularly promising, but the boundless love and grace of God revealed in Jesus Christ is sufficient enough that we are bold in speaking in the title of this book of "overflow." Such an abundant harvest comes not from our ingenuity but from God's power. We must always be careful to remember that while we may do the planting and watering, the growth always comes from God (1 Corinthians 3:6).

ONE SIZE DOES NOT FIT ALL

There are many things that farmers across the world have in common. They understand one another and are always anxious to learn from one another. However, how they practice farming "back home" is shaped uniquely to fit the "lay of the land" where they live. Climate, type of land, and rainfall are just a few of the variables that determine not only the crops they seek to grow but also how they grow them. There may be a few universal truths, but most lessons of farming need to be adapted to local circumstances.

Our hope for you as a reader is that you will take what you read here and not ask, "How do I replicate this in my church?" but rather, "What clue does this idea provide that fits my situation?" It is tempting to think that most innovative ideas require a larger church than ours to accomplish. Many smaller churches cannot do exactly what some larger churches do, but the smallest of churches can find a way to incorporate the spirit or intent of these practices. We illustrate with a practice that some assume can be done only by larger churches.

Of all the things we call church members to do, usually there is only one that we record with precision. Almost all members can ask of their churches, "How much money did I contribute last year?" and receive an answer. Somehow, the smallest and largest of churches manage to put in place systems to care for this indicator

13

of stewardship. But there are relatively few people who can ask of their churches, "How often did I attend worship last year?" and receive an accurate answer. If we say that worship is important (as well as other practices), you would think we would put in place ways to help people see indicators of that stewardship as well.

Some churches, usually large or very large, do have systems in which virtually all who worship record their attendance and then staff or volunteers enter the information so that attendance is tracked about as accurately as giving. For many churches, such systems appear to be unworkable for one or more reasons. In some churches, asking what feels like "the same few" every Sunday to sign an attendance sheet does not fit the culture of the church. In other churches, where it is common practice to distribute a sign-in pad, nothing is done with the information except to identify visitors. Most churches in the United States tend to be smaller churches, and these are the very churches that think putting in place such a "system" that will tell them how often people attend is impossible. Just the opposite is the case. It probably should not be done the way large churches do it. But what if there were one person or a small group of people who know the congregation well and would take a few minutes after worship to check off from a pre-printed list of constituents those present that Sunday? Of course, the goal is not simply to *have* the information but to *use* it. One church that began such tracking had thought of themselves as a church of about twenty-five people who come most Sundays. It turned out that their twenty-five attendees came from a group three times that size. Some follow-up steps permitted them to increase attendance significantly.

Lay and clergy leaders know that one size does not fit all. They also learn to know their context and develop the skills to "translate" clues from one setting into what is appropriate for their congregations. That is our hope for all who are reading this book—so that they can increase participation in vital and life-changing worship, resulting in more people becoming and growing as Christian disciples.

CHAPTER 1

WHY WORSHIP MATTERS

Why do we engage in the act of worship? Why should others? Why should we care about whether others worship?

Most of us are not likely to think about those questions very often. Many of us lead or participate in worship multiple times each month, perhaps even each week. That is a great deal of worship by conventional US patterns today.

But *why* do we worship? Why do some of us see worshiping as so normal that we do not even think about it? It is like wearing a seat belt in an automobile. We do not need to hear a reminder about seat belt safety in order to buckle up. We just do it. In fact, the time when we really notice is when we do not do it.

But worship? Why do we worship?

WORSHIP IS GOD'S CALL UPON OUR LIVES

Tom's wife, Karen, is in a women's Bible study. They decided some time ago to read the Bible in ninety days. That is not easy. Before long, Karen was in the doldrums of the Pentateuch, searching for some faint breeze that would carry her through Deuteronomy. She looked up and said, "I'll tell you one thing: God is serious about worship. I never realized how many commandments there are about what to worship and what not to worship."

Tom was intrigued by her assessment and started doing his own reading. He was likewise surprised when reminded how often the people of God are commanded to worship.

When Moses went to Pharaoh, Moses was not asking for freedom, better working conditions, or a host of other things dealing with simple fairness. Those would have been logical requests given the condition of his people. Notice the subject of his request?

> Our God says to let us go so that we can worship God in the wilderness.

This is the repeated request in Exodus 7, 8, 9, and 10. And Pharaoh says many times, "No."

Why did Pharaoh deny the request that seemed innocent enough? After all, was not Moses' request simply to worship? Perhaps we think that Pharaoh was just stubborn or hardhearted as he reflexively denied all requests for concessions. That may very well have been the case.

But maybe Pharaoh was very astute and had a much more calculated reason for his denials. If the people stay in Egypt, they are *his* people. If they go to the desert and worship, they become *God's* people. Maybe Pharaoh knows that worship is powerful, and if you let your slaves worship God, they may find freedom in all its forms. Pharaoh may have known that worship can be an act of liberation and sedition.

Once the people get out in the desert to worship, God will teach them what to worship and what not to worship. Look at the Ten Commandments. Two of them, a full 20 percent of the whole list, address worship.

> You shall not make for yourself an idol...you shall not bow down to them or worship them...
> Observe the Sabbath day and keep it holy.

God's instruction continues as the children of Israel amble about the wilderness.

> You must not worship the LORD your God in their way, because in worshiping their gods, they do all kinds of detestable things the LORD hates. They even burn their sons and daughters in the fire as sacrifices to their gods. (Deuteronomy 12:31)

Is worship of idols so powerful that it could corrupt someone so deeply?

Such language is found across the Hebrew Bible. This commandment to worship is in Joshua, 1 and 2 Kings, and the prophets, and in even more inspiring forms in the Psalms, where one can almost hear the unity of God's assembled people in the rhythm of Temple liturgy that flows in the poetry.

> Ascribe to the LORD, you heavenly beings,
> ascribe to the LORD glory and strength.
> Ascribe to the LORD the glory due [God's] name;
> worship the LORD in the splendor of [God's] holiness.
> (Psalm 29:1–2)

By the time we reach the writings of the New Testament, devotion to weekly worship in the synagogue and Temple has reached the status of an assumption of the devout life.

So we see that the commands to worship are clear. But why? What is it about worship that leads God to command and require it of us? Despite the practice of a majority of Christians, regular weekly worship is not an option if we are to be faithful people of God. For disciples of Jesus Christ, ignoring worship is simply not acceptable from God's perspective.

But why does God *command* it? Does God have ego issues? You may have had bosses who demand that everything revolve around them. Their sense of entitlement requires that nothing can happen without their approval. Does God want our worship

17

to assuage an Almighty ego? No. The reason is that routinely God says through biblical writers words to this effect:

> I am grateful for your praise. I appreciate the offering. But I already have everything. And, many things you think are valuable are not that important to me.

Worship, then, is a matter of the heart, not simply the heart of God, but the human heart, the seat of our will and the relationships we hold dear.

Perhaps the power of our worship is not primarily for God's sake, but for our sake. Maybe our immutable, unchangeable God is trying to use the power of worship to change us! Could God be trying to transform our lives and make our character more like the character of our God? Can worship be the key to the full sanctification of God's people?

Just how does that work?

WHAT YOU WORSHIP IS WHAT YOU BECOME

Worship is about humility and proximity. When we worship, we come into God's presence and declare God as God. Like people sitting in a cathedral, we are right-sized before God. The proximity helps as we place ourselves in a tight orbit around the most good and righteous being in the Universe. That intimacy transforms us. Have you ever noticed how people who are very invested in their animals may start looking like their pets over time? Have you ever noticed how older couples sometimes grow closer in appearance? It is as if they have been together so long that they are rubbing off on each other.

That is part of the power of worship. It is the exposure to the beauty of God in Christ. That is why we have to pay attention to the fact that in our culture, committed people today are attending less, and uncommitted people do not even show up at Christmas and Easter anymore. It is as if we harassed them for coming only at Christmas and Easter for so long they finally said, "Fine, we'll just sleep in and then enjoy lunch."

But again, does it matter? Is there a consequence of not attending worship each week? Does it matter when parents drive past the sanctuary on their way to do homage at the high altar of sports? We think so. There is something missing in the character development of children who have never met the Good Samaritan, learned the Golden Rule, heard a prophet rail against injustice, bowed their heads in prayer, felt their spirits soar in a hymn of praise, known the community of a crowded pew, or experienced the poetry of the Psalms. The soul and character of a human are the weaker for such neglect. Such children are less equipped for the journey of life that will take them through the troubled waters of ethical dilemmas, to vistas muddled by the fog of uncertainty, up mountains of adversity, and by dry stream beds of fatigue that come to every life. In those moments, God is our provision. Without communion with God, what do we have? These children will soon grow into adults without the rich resources they need to live a fruitful life.

The power of worship can be seen in the temptation of Christ in Matthew 4:9. Satan takes Jesus to a high mountain where he has a view of cities and kingdoms. "All this I will give you," Satan said, "if you will bow down and worship me." Why does Satan not ask Jesus to serve him or obey him? Satan asks for worship.

The consequences of accepting Satan's offer may not seem very serious in a culture where worship is seen as one option among many on any given weekend. What is the big deal? Isn't it *just* a worship service? Nor does worship seem so important in congregations where worship is done with little thought and preparation and where no one seems to expect that lives will be changed by its power.

Satan wants Jesus to bow down and worship him because

19

Satan wants Jesus to offer what people in the Middle Ages called fealty. Fealty was an oath of faithfulness. It was far more than simple obedience. It extended well beyond following orders. It was a pledge of allegiance between a vassal and a person of much higher rank, whose title was lord. This pledge carried the weight of a relationship that included loyalty and alliance that changed the person's identity and life. There were some benefits to the vassal, such as the use of protected land for farming, or other resources of the lord's estate. However, the lord's life was relatively unaltered. For the vassal, these benefits were procured only through a fundamental change of life. The vassal was bound to the lord and the lord's land and directives for the rest of the vassal's life through this oath. Likewise, the vassal's fealty to the lord had a profound effect on the circumstance and identity of the family.

This is why Jesus rejects Satan's offer so quickly: "Away from me, Satan! For it is written: 'Worship the Lord your God, and serve him only'" (Matthew 4:10). Jesus knew that to worship Satan was to alter inexorably his identity, loyalties, and life direction.

Our lives are similarly transformed for good when we worship and serve God only. The apostle Paul states this clearly in Romans 12:

> Therefore, I urge you, brothers and sisters, in view of God's mercy, to offer your bodies as a living sacrifice, holy and pleasing to God—this is true worship. Do not conform to the pattern of this world, but be transformed by the renewing of your mind. (Romans 12:1–2)

WORSHIP IS THE GATEWAY TO RESTORATION

Prophets, after the fall of Judah, speak of a time when people will be restored from their exile. They use the phrase *in that day* to describe a future restoration that God will make of their lives and nation:

> And in that day a great trumpet will sound. Those who were perishing in Assyria and those who were exiled in Egypt will come and worship the LORD on the holy mountain in Jerusalem. (Isaiah 27:13)

In these passages, restoration is connected to the act of worship. It results from what happens when people encounter God in worship.

Kathy's son died two years ago, when he was eighteen, after a protracted series of cancer treatments. It was very sad for everyone in her congregation. Family and friends grieved his death, and Kathy mourned with such a deep love that perhaps only a mother can understand. She entered what the Psalmist calls "the Pit," that hollow space where there is no real consolation. Even now, two years later, she says that the gloom of her lament still reaches out and draws her in. Sunday evening worship in her church includes the weekly celebration of Holy Communion. There are votive candles that worshipers may light after they receive the sacrament and kneel for a time of prayer. Kathy says that there are some weeks, when she is feeling that emptiness, that she comes not for the well-rehearsed music or the insights of the sermon, but to simply receive the sacrament of Holy Communion, to kneel in silence, and then to light a candle. She says that these humble acts have the power to reset her week. It is the presence of Christ that begins to fill the empty space. While the pain of her loss endures, she has stepped toward a more redemptive *in that day* in her life where God is restoring her with moments of joy and allowing her to take the next faithful step into her future.

This ordinary worship is power. It is the power of restoration.

WORSHIP IS THE BASIS OF CHRISTIAN COMMUNITY

One of the most inspiring passages in the journey of Israel occurs after Joshua has led the people to settle the Promised Land. Joshua is an old man and at the end of his life. He has seen it all by this time—the first battles fought by a group of former Egyptian slaves against well-organized enemies, the infidelity of the people, the miracles of God's protection and provision in the desert, the death of Moses, and the conquests that secured Israel's future. Joshua gathers the tribes one last time before sending them to their allotted areas. In the course of this speech, he reminds them of God's faithfulness and their idolatry. He recounts God's goodness and their ingratitude. He speculates that they will never be truly faithful to God. Then he lays out a challenge that is focused on the question of whom they will worship and serve in the future:

> Now fear the LORD and serve him with all faithfulness. Throw away the gods your ancestors worshiped beyond the Euphrates River and in Egypt, and serve the LORD. But if serving the LORD seems undesirable to you, then choose for yourselves this day whom you will serve, whether the gods your ancestors served beyond the Euphrates, or the gods of the Amorites, in whose land you are living. But as for me and my household, we will serve the LORD. (Joshua 24:14–15)

Joshua understood that if they were going to remain a community that was bound together, their center would have to be the worship of their God. Nothing else would have the power to overcome their divided loyalties or call them to a common purpose like a continued relationship with the God who had brought them out of slavery and into a land with houses they did not build and vineyards they did not plant. A new and formidable challenge awaited the children of Israel: prosperity, which is an idol humans have always been willing to worship. The wealth of the land and the gods that the local people believed provided it had the potential to divide them quickly as each clan, having lived for years in scarcity, clamored to serve itself and take hold of its own. The genius of Joshua was to recognize that worship and service are intertwined. Before they went their own ways, they had to commit to their common service of God. If they did not come to this agreement, they would never stand together as a nation. Joshua states clearly what he and his household plan to do, and invites the others to join him. As the speech continues, he challenges their stated ability to worship and serve God. In the end, he seals this as a covenant before all go their own way.

Those who come to worship God today are also looking for community. Too often, the focus of worship is about the individual's experience and each person's individual relationship with God. This is not the nature of biblical worship, which has a focus on the horizontal nature of community as well as our vertical relationship with God. Our life together is experienced when we offer our praise and thanksgiving to God, when we confess our sins in common humility, and when our diverse voices blend into a harmonious offering to God. Sharing sacred space together and dedicating ourselves to serve Christ all work to bring us unity and identity. This is why even the weekly announcements, as banal as they can be some Sundays, are a part of worship. They often invite members of the church to participate in acts of service and fellowship where people come to know one another, forge friendships, and engage in ministry that will be far more significant in the chorus of community than it could have ever been by the isolated effort of the individual.

When the church Tom serves was in the process of planning a new sanctuary, there were many questions raised about the look and feel of the new worship space. One day, Jeff, who is Jewish and married to a woman who is a Christian, and who attends worship every week, pulled Tom aside with a question that was

23

delivered in an urgent tone. "In the fellowship hall where we worship now, we sit in chairs. In the new sanctuary, will there be chairs or pews?"

The decision had not been made. Tom asked, "Which do you prefer?"

Jeff did not hesitate. "You have to go with pews. Pews are church furniture. You sit in chairs; you have defined space. People don't cross the line between chairs. They keep to themselves. You sit in a pew; everybody gets in each other's zone. You sit together, the rich and poor, the liberals and conservatives, and you have to acknowledge that no matter who you are or where you come from, during the worship service, we are all God's children."

When Tom shared Jeff's thoughts with the building committee, they chose pews.

What we talk, sing, and pray about in worship has the power to bring us together as the people of God, a distinct people living, in the words of the hymn, as *pilgrims in this barren land*. Worship matters because it helps us to see the world as it is, ourselves as we are, and the Reign of God as we might experience it if we would grow together in the ways of Christ and long for obedience to his teaching.

Simple, a series of worship services at the church Tom serves, focused the congregation on the materially simple life Jesus taught and exemplified. It was accompanied by a weekly challenge offered at the end of each service. Members of the church were invited to examine their calendars to see how their time was being spent and whether they had created time to attend to their relationships with Christ, their families, and their friends. Classes on budgeting and financial management were offered so that members of small groups could encourage one another in using money wisely, planning for the future, and giving. A *clean-out challenge* was facilitated by the church—offering an industrial document shredder, electronics recycler, trucks from local charities to pick up gently used goods, and a group of teenagers who would refurbish old bikes to be given to children in need. More than 250 cars dropped off load after load of "stuff" on a crisp Saturday morning in October.

The event created a broad conversation among members of the congregation who agreed that having less stuff felt like freedom. It was a giant object lesson in materialism. The combination of challenges, culminating with the use of an estimate-of-giving card as a spiritual practice, enabled the congregation to see that they were a part of something far bigger than the annual pledge drive. The congregation experienced the themes of weekly worship through scripture readings, music, and testimonies from church members who work as personal organizers, as well as through the owner of a removal company called 1-2-3 Junk. Together, these worship experiences gave insights into our longing for things, and the reasons people buy and retain things they no longer use.

Surrounded by other people who nod their heads in agreement, or who later share that they were confronted or inspired by what they heard or what the Spirit said to them in worship, people realize that the congregation is on a journey of sanctification together. Such a journey is best taken in community rather than as individual travelers. Like Joshua, we understand that if God is at our center, we will be able to live the distinct lifestyle to which Christ calls us. Weekly worship is necessary to such a life, however, because the temptation to follow the patterns and values of the surrounding culture are simply too difficult to resist without the constant reinforcement of communal values and identity that worship provides.

WORSHIP IS AN OPPORTUNITY TO REACH NEW DISCIPLES

Worship is a key opportunity for those who are already within a community of faith to invite their family and friends. Many Christians, whether they attend mainline denominations or

25

independent community churches, are far more likely to share an invitation to attend worship than a verbal testimony of how Christ has changed their lives. While there are many side doors into the life of a congregation, from small group Bible studies to service in the local community in which members might invite their friends to participate, no invitational door is wider or opened more frequently than the ones that lead into the sanctuary.

It is essential that those who plan and design worship do so with these invitations in mind. This is the reason that many preachers have begun using thematic series to organize sermon delivery. Sermon series give church members the opportunity to invite people to receive something they may not find elsewhere. Consider a person who is going through the hardship of a painful divorce. He shares with his co-worker that he is having a hard time forgiving his ex-spouse for some of the things she said and did during the divorce proceedings. Now imagine that the co-worker is able to say, "You know, our pastor is starting a sermon series on forgiveness this Sunday. The first week is called 'Why is it so hard to forgive?' Week two is called 'Taking the first steps of forgiveness.' Why don't you come with me this week and see if it would be helpful?"

Now imagine that the same co-worker simply invited his friend to church by saying, "Why don't you come to church with me sometime? I think you will like it."

The first invitation implies that the church will benefit the person being invited. The second invitation may imply that the church needs the benefit of the person.

If the worship service is to reach and help form people as new disciples of Jesus Christ, it must deal honestly with what many have come to call the "cringe factor" common to worship services. Tom first heard this phrase used at a large teaching church. The cringe factor occurs when church members take the risk of asking a friend to join them at a worship service. Many positive things about the church and the worship service experienced by church members could have inspired them to make this invitation. Typically, North American Christians are spiritually shy, and such an invitation to someone who does not attend church is experienced as a social risk. For the love of Christ and the good of their friends, church members invite them to attend worship. But on this Sunday, members notice that while other members are greeted warmly, visitors are rarely spoken to at all. The choir, rather than sharing a well-rehearsed anthem, shares a song that demonstrates how many missed practice that week. The pastor seems to have given too much time to administrative matters in the church and too little to the preparation of the sermon. The sound system pops and emits the high infidelity of feedback. Each time one of these things happens, the church members cringe and ask, "Why did we invite our friends this week!?"

It would be unrealistic to think that every service would enjoy the warmth of Christmas Eve or the power of Easter. However, with regular preparation, planning, and review, worship can become an opportunity for congregations to leverage the simplest and most effective evangelism available: the invitation of their members to their friends.

WHY WORSHIP?

God calls God's people to gather for worship—and to worship God alone. God commands us to worship only God, for by pledging our faithfulness solely to God, we are transformed and grow toward the reflection of the One we worship. Like those exiles long ago, we are restored to new life in worship. And through worship, we are bonded into a community of faith—upholding one another through the power of the Spirit and welcoming others whose lives would be enriched by the journey we are making.

Why worship? God's people cannot live and grow as faithful disciples apart from worship, and those who do not yet know the good news of the Gospel will be unlikely to hear it.

Pay Attention to Those You Seek to Reach

Paying Attention as a Spiritual Discipline

We are all busy in our churches doing good things, but in most of our churches all this activity is not connecting more people to the love of God through our congregations. So it just might be worthwhile for us to pause regularly to pay attention. Some have referred to paying attention as a spiritual discipline. It certainly is a practice that honors those to whom we are giving attention. If we are to reach more people through worship, some serious paying attention is in order.

And our paying attention needs a new orientation.

"Outside to Inside" Thinking

Often, churches practice "inside to outside" thinking. They begin with "this is who we are and what we do" and then seek to promote the church to any who want what we have to offer.

On the other hand, an "outside to inside" perspective begins by thinking of worship from the perspective of those you are seeking to reach—those who are not a part of your church, those who are not attending, those you most hope to reach. Ask yourself: What are their questions? What are their concerns? What are their values? Then, you will better be able to plan your worship out of your own values and traditions and also in a way that will be more responsive to the needs of others.

Many people say they want to reach more people but often never expect to have to make any changes for that to happen. They are not likely to succeed. This is particularly true in seeking to reach younger persons. A survey found that church members want more young people, but, at the same time, they indicated an unwillingness to change their worship or budgets to do so. No wonder we are not more fruitful.

PAYING ATTENTION TO THOSE AROUND YOU

The pastor of a downtown church in a large city recently said, "Are there times when it feels as if your church resides on a different planet than it once did? The street signs are the same. The trees have been there for ages. The sun rises in the morning and the moon at night. But, somehow, everything else feels unfamiliar."

More and more churches are finding themselves in such a situation. All the things they counted on in the past to replenish the church with new generations seem to have broken down. And even within the congregation itself, what used to work no longer has the same power.

The temptation for a church in such times is to turn inward and become more of a members-focused organization and to turn away from its earlier identity as an outwardly focused, mission-centered church.

Thriving congregations focus outwardly on their contexts

while declining congregations increasingly turn their primary attention inward toward current member preferences rather than what might be needed to make their church more welcoming for those who need its message and ministry. Nowhere is this more evident than in worship.

Lovett remembers on some occasions going to a church as the new pastor and being asked, "Pastor, what is your order of worship?" There was an assumption that he had a distinctive order of worship and that the church's worship would now reflect that order.

Other times, someone upon his arrival as the new pastor would give him a recent bulletin and say, "Pastor, this is our order of worship," with the clear expectation that nothing would change.

These two illustrations often represent the two ends of a continuum on which many of the worship debates play out in congregations.

On the one hand, the pastor's values, ideas, and knowledge need to be reflected in the congregation's worship practice. On the other hand, the values and traditions of the congregation need to be honored.

But there is often a missing participant in these discussions—the person for whom your church was established to reach and the person not yet there. The new "outside to inside" thinking required for our new context means we must find ways to involve those not yet there in our worship planning.

Some churches address this by having someone join the worship planning team for the sole purpose of keeping the planning sensitive to those who will be present for the first time. Others are careful to involve at least some persons in the planning who are relatively new themselves to the church.

The goal should always be to develop worship practices that bring together historical, theological, and pastoral considerations in a way that builds current disciples and *reaches those who most need the power of God's love in Christ.*

PLANNING WORSHIP FROM "OUTSIDE TO INSIDE"

It is not easy for those missing people in our communities to influence our planning—even when we have the best of intentions. The congregation is often not a good source for understanding those outside the church. In many cases, churches have become far different from the culture around them and are unrepresentative of those they are seeking to reach. Church people are more likely to be older, married or formerly married, and better off economically, for example, than those outside the church.

Furthermore, the most active church leaders are the least equipped to see the church as those outside do. The longer you have been around, the harder it is to experience your church as an outsider. So if you have been in your church for a while, even if only a matter of weeks, then it is increasingly difficult for you to have an outsider's perspective.

So, what can we do? One approach is to acknowledge our limits and convert them into an advantage.

Think about how you can engage some people on the periphery of your church or outside your church who would be willing to help identify first impressions and clues to help you see things from less of an insider's perspective. Some can even invite friends who do not attend your church to come and "help us learn" more about ourselves from the perspective of the newcomer.

You might also consider practicing what some call "reverse mentoring." In traditional mentoring, the mentor is normally older and more experienced than the person being mentored. In reverse mentoring, those who tend to be older and more experienced ask for help from those younger and with less experience. Here is how it might work for worship planning.

Over the course of the next year, your worship committee

or worship planning team could invite a series of small groups of people to meet with you so you can learn from them. Especially invite those more represented in the broader community than in your congregation. For most churches, this will include younger people, both youth and young adults, but probably not in the same sessions. But these "focus group"-type sessions can include at various times those who recently started attending or those who are different in some way from the majority of the congregation.

Using a few open-ended questions, you will learn much about how others see your church's worship. Ask such things as:

- What means the most to you about worship at this church?

- How is our worship similar to or different from that of other churches you have attended?

- What would improve our worship?

- If there is anything about our worship you would never change, what is it?

- If there is anything you could change, what is it?

There must be strict ground rules for your worship group before the sessions begin. As you ask questions of those you have invited, there are only two things that your group will do. You will *listen* and then *say, "Thank you."* You will repeat this process for the entire conversation period. No one will debate, argue, instruct, or explain. Any sign of defensiveness destroys the purpose of the exercise. There will be plenty of time after the session for the planning group to explore how they can be responsive (not reactive) to what they have heard.

33

PAY ATTENTION TO THE KINDS OF PEOPLE YOU ARE REACHING AND WHO IS MISSING

A question Lovett found helpful as a pastor was, "When we worship on Sunday, who is missing?" In other words, who are the people God has given us (those who live in our communities) who are not represented in our worship in proportion to their presence in the population?

We will cover later the crucial task of carefully tracking attendance numbers, but here the focus is on paying attention to the types of people in your community who are underrepresented in your worshiping community. You may want to begin by seeing if you are missing any of the groups that are most typically missing from congregations to discover if there is one or more that need special attention. Give special attention to any groups whose numbers have been trending downward in recent years.

Types of people most likely to be *less* present in worship than in the community tend to include the following:

- Young adults

- Singles

- Racial and ethnic groups different from the church majority

- Youth

- Children

- Men

Keep in mind that low numbers in any group make it less likely that others like them will participate. That is where small changes in their presence can make a big difference. The focus

34

you give to a particular category of people at one time is not because they are more important than others but because all people are important, and these just happen to be the ones at this time who need the attention. It is a bit like the good shepherd's concern for the one missing sheep even though there were many more sheep not missing.

Once you decide on the group to which you should pay special attention, count the number of such people in worship each week. Some person or group needs responsibility for the project. Careful monitoring of those attending will help you understand who they are and any common traits they have. It should trigger ways to connect with them, involve them, and to learn things important to them. At first, it may be hard to have many if you are starting from a low or even nonexistent base. But even modest steps that result in just a few more people attending in a particular category can, over time, become a change that begins to build on itself.

Keep in mind that the degree of presence of people in the categories named above tends to be associated with growing churches. Growing churches pay attention not only to those who show up but also to those who are not there.

Two exercises can help your congregation plan worship with sensitivity toward new people you are trying to reach.

What Do People in Your Community Care About?

Think of people in your community who do not attend your church or other churches—people with whom you work, your neighbors, your children's classmates, etc. Now, discuss these questions to the best of your ability with one important guideline—*avoid any negative or judgmental language because this is not likely how they view themselves.*

1. What are their concerns?

2. What do they value?

3. What are their questions?

At the conclusion of the exercise, allow time for participants to share their responses with one another.

Exchange Visitors to Learn How New People Experience Your Church

In this exercise, two churches agree to exchange visitors to get feedback from people unfamiliar with your church. They simply agree to ask from two to five of your members to visit the other church in exchange for some of the other church's members visiting your worship service. The exchange does not have to be on the same Sunday.

When the visitors are selected, give them the "Visitor Feedback Survey" provided below.

When the visitors attend worship, they will complete the Visitor Feedback Survey and submit it to a designated person from the church visited. The person receiving the form need not be in a formal leadership position but does need to be seen as objective and credible among congregational leaders. This person will take the feedback forms and compile a list of observations and suggestions coming from the visitors.

The resulting report can then be shared with congregational leaders so they can address this question: What did we learn from this exercise to improve how people experience worship?

VISITOR FEEDBACK SURVEY

Name of church visited: _____

_____

Date of service attended: _____

Time of service: _____

Skip any questions that do not apply.

The numbered scale goes from lowest score (1) to highest (5).

Pre-Service Outside:

Appearance and availability of parking:
1   2   3   4   5

Visitor parking provided?
Yes   No

Cleanliness and appearance of exterior:
1   2   3   4   5

Directional signage:
1   2   3   4   5

Was location of the nursery evident?
Yes   No

Pre-Service Inside:

Promptness of greeting by others:
1   2   3   4   5

Friendliness of greeters:
1   2   3   4   5

Helpfulness of greeters:
1   2   3   4   5

Bulletin appearance and helpfulness:
1   2   3   4   5

Visitor packet provided?
Yes No

Cleanliness & appearance of narthex/reception area:
1   2   3   4   5

Cleanliness of restrooms:
1   2   3   4   5

Appearance of sanctuary:
1   2   3   4   5

Service:

Easily understood order of worship:
1   2   3   4   5
Appropriate and effective music:
1   2   3   4   5

Sermon effectiveness:

1   2   3   4   5

Prayers:

1   2   3   4   5

Energy and engagement of worshipers:

1   2   3   4   5

Sound sufficient to hear easily:

1   2   3   4   5

Seating comfort:

1   2   3   4   5

Temperature:

1   2   3   4   5

Post Service:

Were you greeted after the service?
Yes No

Were you invited to return to church?
Yes No

Were you invited to a fellowship or study opportunity after worship?
Yes No

Overall Comments:

What did you notice first? _____

_____

_____

What did you like best? _____

_____

_____

What would have made the experience better?_____

_____

_____

What features of this experience would make you more likely to come again if you lived nearby? _____

_____

_____

What features of this experience would make you less likely to come again if you lived nearby? _____

_____

_____

Other comments: _____

_____

_____

_____

_____

_____

PAY ATTENTION TO WORSHIP SERVICES

PAY ATTENTION TO WORSHIP PLANNING

Careful attention to the planning of worship is critical if services of worship are to be faithful opportunities to witness to the Gospel of Jesus Christ. Many churches, we have discovered, need to place a much higher priority on such planning. A major study across all US religious groups found that one thing that distinguishes mainline denominational churches from other churches is that much less time is spent on the planning and preparation for worship services.

Pastor Nelson Searcy reminds us, "If you don't pay close attention to the details of your worship service, they will atrophy."[1] Some worship planning characteristics of growing churches are that

- they spend much time in planning for worship long term and weekly,

- they prepare extensively for each service, and

- they regularly evaluate and revise what they are doing.

Our task is neither to copy someone else's way of worshiping nor to defend everything we are now doing. Instead, it is to examine prayerfully and thoughtfully our worship in a way that connects a growing number of people with God's love through Jesus Christ.

What is your current worship planning system? Your first response may be, "We don't have one." In reality, every congregation has a planning system, but it may be unintentional and lack focus. The way that worship unfolds each week *is* your planning system. Think about these questions as a way of understanding your system:

1. Who is involved?

2. How far ahead do we plan?

3. How much time is spent?

4. How much communication is there among worship leaders?

5. How do we evaluate our worship services and share feedback each week?

6. How does our planning take into account those we are most seeking to reach?

FIRST, ASSESS WHERE YOU ARE

Before planning for the future, it can help to take time to assess the current state of your worship, especially as experienced by the worshipers. Take a "snapshot" of worship as it is now in order to provide both a baseline and an agenda for your planning.

Pay Attention to Who Is Participating

Church visitors often report that there is high energy from the worship and music leaders but that there is much less energy within the congregation as a whole. It is helpful to remember that liturgy means "the work of the people," not something a few leaders do on behalf of the congregation. Therefore, the participation of the congregation is essential to vital worship. Pay attention to how much engagement you see from those not in leadership roles. This assessment can become a good opportunity to remind choirs that their first responsibility is to encourage and lead congregational singing.

Pay Attention to Who Is Leading

In addition to paying attention to the level of participation occurring among the gathered worshipers, also pay attention to the people who have leadership roles in the service. Whom do people see in front of them during the worship time? Make sure they represent what your vision is as a church and those you hope to reach. Remember that people "hear what they see." In one congregation that is relatively non-diverse by many standards, the scripture was read for a series of many weeks by different persons in the congregation whose first language was not English. The members read a passage in their native language and then in English. There turned out to be quite a few persons in the congregation from those diverse backgrounds, a fact not part of the church's self-perception. That effort changed how the congregation saw itself in a way that statistics never would.

Pay Attention to the Tone of the Service

How would people describe worship at your church? Do they speak of your worship as joyful and uplifting? Pay attention to their descriptions to make sure that they are experiencing a

43

spiritually vital service where they are invited to encounter God. Do their descriptions match the church's identity and calling? Is your worship such that people not only come back, but they invite others to come with them? Some churches discover they are not ready to invite new people. If current members are not inviting others, perhaps that is a clue that you may need to review the tone of your service. If your worship is not so alive and vital that people are drawn to it by its power, then you may need to work first on the worship service and then on inviting others.

Ways to Understand Your Worship Service Better

We know it is hard for us to experience our own church as others do, especially newcomers. We are too familiar with everything. We will share some exercises to help you and others from your church think more thoroughly, systematically, and objectively about your worship by drawing from the insights of worshipers.

In using any of these and other feedback tools, keep in mind that you are looking for clues to improve your worship. You probably will find yourself saying, "I never thought of that" or "I never noticed that before." You want to be responsive without attempting to address every suggestion. Not all things you learn will be useful or appropriate in your context. There will be many more ideas generated than can be implemented immediately.

Worship Video Review

If you already video record your worship, then you have what you need to begin. If not, find someone in the congregation with the equipment and skill to make such recordings. Once you have the video recording, form several groups to view the video and discuss a series of questions for which you want their response. Some examples include the following:

- What went particularly well?

- What could be improved?

- What is not clear?

- What language assumes prior knowledge first-time guests would not have?

- Where are there time gaps?

- Are any things taking too much or too little time?

- What other observations did you have?

Ask each group to submit their reports. Then, ask someone good at organizing information to take all the reports and compile a report for those who plan worship. The task of organizing the learnings should go to someone who can be objective and is not directly involved in worship planning. Simply compiling the verbatim feedback is not helpful.

The goal is to put the feedback in a form that identifies specific suggestions and questions as well as recurring broad themes. The key question becomes, "What did we learn from this exercise to improve how people experience worship?" The response to this question will give your worship planners something with which they can work.

Congregational Survey

This exercise involves administering a brief survey distributed in your worship bulletin. Ask your worshipers to complete the survey. If possible, collect it with the offering in order to achieve maximum participation.

Or, if your church has regular e-mail correspondence with members, you might conduct a worship survey online. There are several relatively inexpensive services for conducting your survey online.

Use a few simple questions. Here are some examples:

1. What aspect of worship means the most to you?

2. If someone asked you to describe worship at your church, what words would you use?

3. If you could change one thing about worship, what would it be?

To organize the results, again it is best to find one or more persons not directly involved in planning worship, but good at taking information and objectively identifying some clues that might improve worship. Typically, some clues will be small and others large.

One reason it does not help to share verbatim results with those closest to worship is that the inevitable negative or caustic comments will loom out of proportion in their minds. It is better to let others work with the raw data, ignoring random remarks for which there is no general pattern of concern.

On the basis of the clues revealed through the survey, those responsible for worship can again consider the question "What did we learn from this exercise to improve how people experience worship?"

Worship Think-Tank Sessions

Pastors and other leaders can convene focus groups or "think tanks" to talk about the purpose of worship and to hear what helps the congregation experience the holiness of corporate worship. Unlike the "reverse mentoring" focus groups discussed in the previous chapter, where the goal is to learn from a particular constituency, think-tank sessions should include a representative sample of the congregation in terms of age, race, musical tastes, and commitment levels. The following sample agenda is offered as a starting point for such a meeting.

WORSHIP THINK-TANK SESSION

1. Invite participants to share a favorite worship song and their earliest memory of attending a worship service.

2. Highlight qualities of worship your congregation seeks to embody. The following are examples and starting points for you to consider:

   - The worship of God is holy: We worship because God is holy and we, the created, worship and serve the creator.

   - Excellence: We bring our finest because we love God.

   - Gladness: Not just an emotion, gladness is a byproduct of joy.

   - Response: Worship is not just an hour on Sunday but a constant response to God.

3. Draw from these questions to elicit important clues about worship at your church:

   - If there are multiple services, what service do you prefer and why? What matters most, style of worship or time of service?

   - When do you crave worship? When do you absolutely make it a priority?

   - Tell about a particularly meaningful worship service at our church or another.

47

- Ask participants to portray their understanding of worship through a drawing. Assure them that talent in art is not required for this activity.

- What is it that helps you be comfortable in worship?

- What makes you "cringe" in worship?

- What makes our worship most meaningful for you?

- What is missing in our current worship services that might help us offer our best worship to God?

The goal of these questions is to allow members of the congregation to share their insights and aspirations with the worship leaders. It is important to begin the conversation in such a way that participants understand that they are not redesigning the worship services or simply offering negative feedback to preachers, musicians, ushers, or artists. The goal of the think tank is to consider together the function of worship, how it glorifies God and enables people to commune with God and neighbor, and to offer insight into how its various components fulfill those goals.

BUILD A WORSHIP TEAM

Since the 2010 earthquake that struck Haiti, hundreds of church groups have traveled to that country to help clear rubble and rebuild homes, medical clinics, schools, and churches. One of the most common experiences of those who have participated in such efforts is the bucket brigade. Large equipment to remove rubble, such as backhoes or bulldozers, is not readily available in Haiti. Things are done the old-fashioned way. A collection of five-gallon plastic buckets is brought to the worksite. Team members make a long line extending from the rubble to the place where it will be moved. On one end, volunteers fill buckets. On the other end, people empty the buckets. In between, people pass buckets from person to person until the rubble is gone. Likewise, the bucket brigade is often utilized to move construction supplies to the work site. Sand, gravel, and water for the cement used in new buildings are often brought a bucket at a time to construction workers eager for materials. Empty buckets are either given to runners who take them back to the beginning or tossed back up the line, joyfully void of their prior burden.

There are few places where the value of fellow team members is experienced any more than the bucket brigade. Every single person is important. The more you have, the more the weight of the work is shared, and the more you accomplish. The fewer you have in the group, the more everyone has to stretch and work harder to cover the distance between the two ends of the brigade. The bucket brigade produces an amazing level of unity among volunteers who may speak different languages and who come from different countries. We are all one on the bucket brigade.

Contrast this experience with the movement from worship planning to the implementation of ideas on any given Sunday in a church. Rather than a bucket brigade, there is often a pastor running from concept to implementation, with an occasional pass to a musician or a last-minute toss to the ushers. Not only is worship less likely to be led in a coordinated and prepared fashion, but there is also the loss of contributions others would make if they had a way to offer their spiritual gifts to the service. Whether working with a church staff or with volunteers, pastors are most likely to lead meaningful worship services when they work well with a team. They will also be able to retain important "people resources" for longer periods of time because the work is shared, and thus the whole church is better served.

Consider the woman who works as a volunteer pianist at her church. She is an eager volunteer who likes to be prepared for worship each week by practicing the music that she will play.

49

She could play the piano in many venues. She has been invited to play for bands that entertain in bars and for parties as well as community groups that sing together. She offered to fill this role in her church because of the joy she feels when she uses her musical gifts and training to glorify God. This role is an act of worship in her life. She would like the congregation to be able to sing hymns that thematically connect to the scripture reading and sermons the pastor will preach, believing that an integrated service will serve the message the pastor has been inspired to share.

She has asked the pastor if he might be able to provide his texts and hymn selections on Monday. When he failed to follow through, she offered to choose the hymns if he would simply provide the weekly texts. The pastor replied that he would not be able to send these until the Thursday prior to Sunday's service. She offered to meet with the pastor quarterly to discuss what themes might be appropriate for various seasons and what hymns he would like the congregation to learn. He promised to get back to her but never followed through. The dispirited volunteer considered leaving her role as accompanist until a friend talked her into staying, noting that she had a great deal of training and interest in worship and sharing how much people in the church appreciated her. This volunteer finally notified the pastor that in order to be prepared, she would simply choose the hymns she wanted to play each week and give them to the secretary in time for the bulletin to be prepared.

Think of the difference in the relationship this key volunteer would have with the pastor if he were willing to consider her part of the team that leads worship each week. Music and message could be coordinated. The volunteer would be honored and appreciated for her commitment. If the pastor is not interested in planning for these reasons, he would be wise to consider the economic cost of replacing this volunteer with someone of similar musical competency. It would require the church to add a part-time employee to the budget and lead the pastor to have to spend more time on financial stewardship.

The ideas presented in this book will seem unrealistic and possibly overwhelming without the benefit of a worship planning team. The good news is that while the leadership of worship planning rests on the pastor in most churches, creative ideas, resources, and implementation of a plan can be the work of many. A worship planning team should include the pastor, a music director, and a chairperson for the team. This chairperson's role might include coordinating greeters, ushers, parking lot greeters, sanctuary stewards, communion servers, and other volunteers who will be present during weekly worship services. It is also helpful to include on the team the person who works with bulletins and communication so that special services and sermon series can be emphasized throughout the congregation. This communications person often chooses relevant graphics for sermon series if video screens and slides are used in the sanctuary. Understanding the place of special services and the theme for a series will enable a designer to prepare materials in ways that reinforce the goals of the services. Other important people to consider for this committee are those known for their creativity. They may include volunteers who have artistic abilities, or those who know how to create videos that might be used in worship. These volunteers should be enlisted especially for their abilities to think creatively rather than for the items they might prepare for the worship experience. Those with creative talents in the visual arts often have a view on the world that enables them to think of ways to enhance themes or see connections that might be missed otherwise. The worship planning process includes the following:

- A preaching plan with a central theme or image, biblical texts, and sermon series descriptions for each week

- Sharing the preaching schedule with team members

- Gathering ideas to improve the sermons and series with themes, artwork, videos, music, and programs that might augment the preaching plan, such as workshops or small group opportunities

- Assignments that enable all the volunteers to understand the goal of the preaching plan and what roles they will take in the service each week

- Weekly planning and evaluation

THE PREACHING PLAN

Planning the sermon series will require an investment of time and effort on the part of the pastor. While initially time intensive, this planning will save the pastor hours in the efficiency it will create throughout the year in sermon preparation and conversation with those involved in worship. Tom has taken a four-day retreat for many years to plan sermon series, often in the spring. It is important to take books, commentaries, and other materials for this time apart that will assist in the process. A retreat is an opportunity for pastors to immerse themselves in reading the Bible and books that will guide their thinking. It should include times of prayer and silence, recognizing that the Holy Spirit is a part of every aspect of worship planning for the year. Before leaving for a retreat, the pastor might use social media or surveys to ask the congregation what topics would be helpful to them in preaching, what books of the Bible they would like to consider in the coming year, and what questions of faith they would like the pastor to address from the pulpit. If working in a multi-staff church, pastors will benefit from a meeting where staff members can share their insights. If the pastor works with limited staff, key leaders can be convened for the same purpose.

Many pastors may prefer to use the lectionary as a guide to

preaching rather than sermon series around a topic or questions. Lectionary preachers can use this planning process in ways that will greatly assist their worship teams by identifying the key texts and themes that will be shared on a given Sunday. If the Gospel text is the primary focus of the sermon, musicians can prepare so that the anthem they select pertains to the Gospel text rather than another scripture reading. No matter how the pastor selects the passages that will focus the weekly sermon, the clarity of advance planning serves the team as a whole well.[2]

The preaching plan should include a title and general description of the sermon series. Dates, followed by texts and possible sermon titles, along with a description of each sermon and key verses, will be very helpful to musicians and choir directors. It is also helpful in relation to other events that will occur on that Sunday such as sacraments, recruitment efforts, and special recognitions that will take place. An example from Tom's church is included at the end of this chapter.

Pastors returning from their planning retreat with 6 to 12 months of Sundays in this form have a powerful tool at their disposal to unify their team and enable everyone to coordinate their efforts with common themes and purposes. The descriptions found in the preaching plan enable musicians, communicators, and creative thinkers on the worship team to understand what the pastor was thinking when spending time alone with God to consider the worship ministry of the church. The next step is to make sure the team is fully included in the planning process.

SHARE THE PLAN

Tom recalls the first time he asked his new choir director if she could make the themes of her weekly anthems match the themes of the weekly sermons. She said that she would be happy to do so. All it would require is that Tom provide her with four months' notice. He initially thought this an unreasonable request. He liked to work week to week or a month at a time at best. He liked the ability to be spontaneous. The choir director affirmed his right to work in any fashion he desired as the pastor. "But if you want the themes of the music to match the sermon, that will require planning," she stated gently.

The choir director walked Tom through her planning process, which began with selecting and ordering music. This was followed by matching music to her rehearsal schedule. Harder pieces of music required more practice time with the choir. High seasons of the church year often had more opportunities for music in worship. After she finished sharing her procedure, Tom understood that four months' notice would be helpful, but six months would make her task easier and take away some of the time pressure she felt. Two months later, when he brought a document that contained nine months of sermon planning, she was appreciative and excited. When they sat down with other members of the worship team and began to refine the plan and consider ways to integrate various components of the weekly worship service, she began to offer ideas that would have remained like buried talents had she not been involved.

The pastor should walk through each section of the preaching plan, giving special attention to the goals of each sermon, series, or liturgical season. This is a summary that will allow other members of the worship team the opportunity to ask questions and clarify what they find in the planning document. This approach gives team members the opportunity to begin their initial thinking and join the pastor in the creative process that will enhance the work of the preaching plan and, more importantly, the worship experience of those attending.

GATHERING MATERIALS

The next step is to have a conversation about how to coordinate and augment each series so that the experience of worship will be vital throughout the year. This work is best done by taking the preaching plan in sections, by series or season of the year. Creative work takes a great deal of energy. It is far easier to consider sections of a six- to twelve-month plan over the course of meetings separated by weeks than to respond to the entire document in one extended session. The pastor may want to lead a brainstorming session on a particular series if her ideas are not yet fully formulated. However, another member of the team may facilitate this discussion so that the pastor can step back and let the team members take more ownership of the thoughts that are shared. If the pastor takes too strong a leadership role, creativity may be stifled rather than enhanced. Ideas from team members may change the series and cause the pastor to reconsider choices he has made. Pastors should not be discouraged if they occasionally have to go back to the drawing board and consider the series again. The group may be saving the pastor from three to four hard weeks ahead if the series falls flat. A test of the team's strength is the level of collegiality necessary to share such honest feedback with the pastor in a thoughtful way.

Team members should look at each series through the lens of their particular roles, but they should also feel free to discuss the series as a whole. Many questions can be asked, including the following:

- What images or symbols would help the congregation access the themes of the sermons?

- How can sermons be enhanced through handouts, outlines, or experiential elements of worship?

- How will the series be supported musically? Are there particular songs or hymns that would be helpful to the congregation?

- Will drama, dance, or visual arts be utilized in some way?

55

- What would make this experience both worshipful and memorable to those who attend?

- Are there books, small group experiences, or workshops that the church might offer to provide more in-depth learning opportunities?

ASSIGNMENTS

When this meeting is concluded, members of the team will need to take on the particular work of their role. Musicians will select music. Graphics can be chosen and copy written for future posts on the church website, newsletters, bulletins, or direct mail pieces. Small group leaders can begin to consider curriculum and leader recruitment. Worship planners will need to work with the various group members to integrate their choices with the preaching plan.

It may sound as though all the team members would joyfully embrace a process that allows them to be prepared and coordinated. However, many of the team members may enjoy the leisure of procrastination and the rush of last-minute planning as much as the pastor once did. For this process to work, the pastor or some other person on the team will need to take a coordinating role for the various inputs required to complete the plan.

Often, it is better to assign this task to a highly organized layperson who is familiar with project planning. Pastors are generalists by vocation. Having returned with the initial preaching plan, pastors discover that many other priorities in the church will claim their attention. And, having spent a great deal of time on their planning retreat, they may feel that the work is done when it has actually just begun. Often, there are church members who have strong administrative gifts that have been developed in other vocations who would enjoy helping their pastor and church by working in a coordinating role between the various parties on the worship team.

It is essential that someone keep the group members account-able to deadlines that will need to be established so that everyone can be informed of the unfolding worship plan throughout the year. This work will enable the team to be more efficient in the weekly preparation for worship services and free of the conflicts that arise when the left hand does not know what the right hand is doing. Clear assignments with clear deadlines, which are all documented in a central location accessible by all team members, is essential for the process to work.

WEEKLY EVALUATION AND PLANNING

A weekly evaluation time is a critical ingredient of the planning process. It allows the team to make course corrections, celebrate one another's gifts and contributions, and communicate ways in which team members can work well together. In churches with a paid staff and multiple services that need to be considered separately, the meeting may be weekly and take an hour. In smaller congregations, the pastor may simply spend time on the phone with one or two volunteers who lead music or coordinate volunteers for the worship service. No matter what size the church, time spent evaluating the week's service is helpful to the goal of a vital worship experience for the congregation.

Some questions used in Tom's church for evaluation of the previous weekend's services:

- What honored God?

- Was Christ lifted up and celebrated?

- Where did you/others encounter God?

- In what ways did worship components offer or hinder the Holy Spirit?

57

- What are the specific action points needed to improve in the future?

Nelson Searcy uses these questions at The Journey Church in New York City:

- What went right?
- What went wrong?
- What was missing?
- What was confusing?

Each question results in a list of responses. Then, assignments are made for those things where someone needs to take action.[3] These two lists of questions focus team members in different ways. One helps the group think theologically. The other enables the group to think pragmatically. Good worship planning works on both the theological and pragmatic axes, but the questions asked may provide different outcomes and results. Some team members will best engage this process if they enter through a theological doorway with a focus on glorifying God and possible personal transformation through worship. Others will feel this evaluation time to be valuable if they see clear changes to the worship plan that come as a result of working through a practical process of feedback, evaluation, and assignments of responsibilities.

Evaluation leads naturally into planning for the next week and beyond. In all our planning, keep in mind the concept of "outside to inside" thinking. By this time in the process, the concern is that attention can all be on those responsible for leading the worship instead of on those who will experience the worship.

Finding ways to keep the worshipers foremost in planning conversations makes it more likely that your worship will be vital, welcoming, and compelling.

Nelson Searcy uses three questions to help focus planning for each service on the worshipers:

• What do we want people to *know* when they leave?

• What do we want people to *feel* when they leave?

• What do we want people to *do* when they leave?[4]

In order to put the coming weekend into the larger planning context, a weekly planning sequence might be similar to the one that follows.

A Long-term View

• Are there actions we need to take now to prepare for the series or season ahead?

The Next Six Weeks

• Review the theme of each service.

• Review the one central image that will communicate each theme.

• What will enhance the communication of the central image and theme of each service?

• Are there problems that need to be solved, items secured, or tasks assigned?

This Coming Sunday

- Remind everyone of the theme and central image of this service.

- Review what is planned that will enhance the communication of the central image and theme.

- Are there problems yet to be solved, items secured, tasks assigned?

- Review the communication plan to make sure that necessary information goes to each person who needs to know (office staff, sound and video operators, greeters/ushers, Communion stewards, and so on).

Final Recap of Assignments

Team members who become comfortable with evaluation and planning will soon learn to share in these tasks quickly and freely, understanding that the feedback offered is not intended as criticism of any team member, but rather reflects a desire to enhance the worship experience. Once this component of the process is embraced, pastors, musicians, and other volunteers of churches will find that they are able to speak to one another briefly before, after, or between (and sometimes even during!) services and make changes to smooth transitions, adjust how worship is led, and even modify sermon content in ways that will further glorify God.

EXAMPLE OF A SERIES PLANNING OUTLINE

Stung by the Tongue:

A Sermon Series from the Book of James

The hurt that can be caused by the tongue can wound us deeply and stick with us for decades. What others say to us and about us really matters, just as it matters what we say to and about others. This series will explore the power of the tongue and give suggestions for how we can be a people who build others up while speaking the truth in love.

September 2 (Communion, Labor Day weekend, elementary school partnership volunteer recruitment)

Title: Corner Criticism

Scripture: James 3:7–12

3:8–9: "[B]ut no one can tame the tongue. It is a restless evil, full of deadly poison. With the tongue we praise our Lord and Father, and with it we curse human beings, who have been made in God's likeness."

Criticism can be hurtful, and we can overcome this by becoming encouragers who can speak the truth in love and affirm the good we see in others. We are called to intentionally encourage rather than carelessly criticize those who are in our lives.

September 9 (Sunday school kick-off)

Title: Harness Hearsay

61

Scripture: James 3:3–6; 4:11–12

3:5b–6: "Consider what a great forest is set on fire by a small spark. The tongue also is a fire, a world of evil among the parts of the body. It corrupts the whole person, sets the whole course of one's life on fire[.]"

Gossip versus assuming the best about others. It is so easy to speak about others in a way that creates rumors and sends out impressions that can never be corrected as they move from person to person. Instead, we are called to assume the best about others and check our facts so that we can correct bad information or innuendo that we hear about others.

September 16

Title: Bind Bitterness

Scripture: James 3:13–18

3:17: "But the wisdom that comes from heaven is first of all pure; then peace-loving, considerate, submissive, full of mercy and good fruit, impartial and sincere."

Bitter words versus merciful messages. It is important that we not correct others in a way that promotes bitterness between us. Instead, the scripture calls us to be honest with each other, giving that last 10 percent, but with care to be tactfully candid. The way we say things is often more important than the point we are trying to make to the other person.

September 23

Title: Growing Gratitude

Scripture: James 5:7–11

5:8–9: "You too, be patient and stand firm, because the Lord's coming is near. Don't grumble against one another, brothers and sisters, or you will be judged."

Griping and grumbling versus gratitude. Most people have circumstances that might lead them to grumble about their lives or other people. James calls us to realize that we will be judged by God for the way we judge others. In order to persevere, we must be grateful for the way God redeems hardship and for the compassion and mercy we enjoy.

September 30 (New Member Sunday)

Title: Dialogue Sermon: Power of Words to Hurt or Heal

The pastors take questions from the congregation related to Christian conversation, the temptation to misuse the tongue, the power of encouragement, and so on.

Pay Attention to Attendance Seasons and Patterns

Attendance Seasons

We are used to thinking of the seasons of the Christian year as Advent, Christmastide, Epiphany, and so forth. There are also attendance seasons that follow common patterns across congregations. It is important to understand these in order to plan for them accordingly.

Big Days

There are two times when attendance surpasses the average, Easter and Christmas Eve. A significant portion of the attendance for the year may occur on just these two occasions. And yet, some churches do not make plans to be attentive to Easter attendance because "we always have a big crowd on Easter." And while some churches do not conduct Christmas Eve services, others are having attendance on Christmas Eve that matches or surpasses Easter. It is essential to maximize these days as ways to reach current participants and new people *and also* to see these services as foundational for building continued attendance through special planning for the periods following these important holidays.

Prime Seasons

Prime seasons are the times of the year when people are most likely to attend in higher numbers than any other times except the two "big days."

One prime season comes in January and February. The busyness of the holiday season has passed, and people are getting back to work and school. They are thinking about starting the new year in a constructive way. It is even possible that taking their spiritual life more seriously was one of their New Year's resolutions. This is the ideal time to invite your Christmas visitors to become active and engaged.

Another prime season is Lent. Church members are often open to doing something different during Lent, such as participating in a class or small group, reading a book tied to a sermon series, or committing to attending worship each week as a Lenten discipline. Some congregations choose a Lenten study curriculum—perhaps tied to a sermon series—for use by all small groups in the church, publicizing it widely to use as a way to recruit new participants into small group study.

The fall period between the beginning of school and November is another prime time. With summer vacations completed, this "back to school" period is a time when parents are likely to be seeking out a Sunday school or other types of activities for their children—and when people of all ages tend to settle into a more regular pattern of engagement.

Advent is another prime time. Non-churchgoers may be more open to reflecting on their faith or their struggles during this season, and they may be more likely to attend church in the time leading up to Christmas than at any other time of year. The key to building attendance in each of these seasons is planning, planning, planning, and doing it well in advance.

Low Times

There are traditional seasons in which attendance in most churches tends to be lower than usual. These times are the post-Easter period and summer. And yet, failing to concentrate on these periods sends the message that they are unimportant, and low attendance becomes a self-fulfilling prophecy. The post-Easter period is a very critical time for engaging those who visit at Easter. And summer is often a time when people will visit churches, particularly as more and more schools and colleges have pushed the beginning of their school year well into August. Churches that maintain a full schedule of worship and programming can be surprised to find that the people they assumed were "on vacation" all summer are in town much more than they had assumed.

ATTENDANCE PATTERNS

One of the key roles of any church leader is to help define reality. Knowing how your church is doing as quickly and accurately as possible is always a key leadership task. So leaders must interpret reality in meaningful ways.

Understanding worship attendance trends is critical to defining reality for congregations because all agree that worship attendance is one primary indicator of congregational vitality. Many other good things tend to follow from strong worship participation. Therefore, keeping attuned to fluctuations in attendance can give leaders important clues.

Unfortunately, however, churches do not often maintain worship statistics in ways that facilitate the most helpful comparisons and, thus, analyses. Most churches collect weekly attendance data and report it to the congregation. The most common practice is to report attendance for the previous week. Sometimes there will be a comparison with the same Sunday a year ago. Neither of these practices provides helpful information about trends and patterns. Often, the circumstances of any one Sunday—be it weather related, special days, or memorial observances—make any such comparisons meaningless.

52-Week Rolling Average Concept

We invite you to consider what may be for you a new way to think about tracking worship attendance—monitoring worship attendance by using a 52-week rolling average (hereafter referred to as 52-week average). By calculating a 52-week average after each Sunday, you have a better representation of the broad array of highs and lows that are present each year.

With the more typical methods of reporting attendance, you could notice a single week having high or low attendance without being able to put that number in a larger perspective. Using a 52-week average helps you see how you are doing relative to the entire past year, realizing that this "basket of weeks" will contain both Easter and summertime as well as other high and low times. Therefore, you can see longer-term patterns that are not apparent by looking at the attendance for any single Sunday or month.

The Lewis Center for Church Leadership developed the Congregational Attendance Profile (CAP)[1] to measure and compare attendance patterns on a 52-week average. Quite a few congregations are now using this tool as they review attendance. The pastor of one church where the staff met every Monday morning reports that before using the Congregational Attendance Profile, staff spirits were either high or low each week based on the Sunday attendance report. When attendance was high, everyone felt that "things are really coming together." When attendance was low, it was easy to fall into the "nothing is working" mindset.

The Congregational Attendance Profile put the highs and lows in a larger and more realistic context.

Throughout the year, regardless of season, this resource helps provide an accurate picture of how you are doing relative to the past year as a whole. While changes in attendance patterns do not occur quickly, the sooner you identify such changes, the better able your church will be to respond appropriately.

How It Works

The Lewis Center developed the Congregational Attendance Profile not only to enable churches to keep attendance records in a way that calculates a 52-week average, but, even more importantly, to give tools to learn from trends and to improve worship attendance. Whether you are using the formatted templates provided by the CAP or designing your own spreadsheets, the task is to record your weekly attendance for the past two years in order to give the data needed to calculate an ongoing 52-week average. Each week, one week's attendance is dropped to make room for the new "52nd Sunday" in the new calculation. If you have multiple services, you probably will want to record and calculate averages for each individual service as well as for the combined attendance at all services.

The important work, however, is not in capturing and recording the data but in using the data to discern clues from your church's attendance patterns in order to strengthen attendance.

Attendance Seasons and Week-by-Week Fluctuations

Once your attendance data are entered, the CAP will produce charts that can help you understand your overall attendance trends as well as your seasonal attendance patterns throughout the year. Again, you can create these charts yourself if you design your own instrument.

The chart that churches find most helpful for their planning places weekly attendance for the past year over the 52-week running average for the current year. Looking at your weekly attendance in this way can be quite revealing. Some churches have shown major improvement in attendance by acting on lessons learned from such a chart. We have examples from two churches that have been using this process.

For these charts, you will notice how the churches have drawn vertical lines to mark certain times and seasons of the year. It is useful to mark important dates in the life of your church. Note Easter, Christmas, back to school, Advent, Lent, and summer. Take note of other significant dates on your church calendar: Confirmation, homecoming, Sunday school kick-off, or any other special worship celebrations unique to your church.

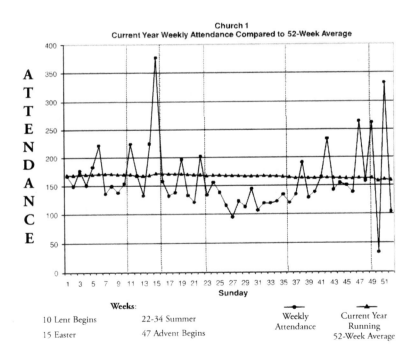

Church 1
Current Year Weekly Attendance Compared to 52-Week Average

Weeks:		Weekly Attendance	Current Year Running 52-Week Average
10 Lent Begins	22-34 Summer		
15 Easter	47 Advent Begins		

70

In the chart for Church 1, there are some recurring patterns that will probably hold true for your church as well:

- You will find that there are many Sundays for which the attendance falls below the 52-week average. Of course, there must be Sundays below average—but often people are surprised by how many there are.

- That leads to another realization about how important a few Sundays are, especially Easter. Easter accounts for far more of your annual average than you might realize.

- You can see that many churches' attendance patterns reveal the pattern described earlier as "big days," "prime seasons," and "low times."

Now, we can look more closely at the two churches and note what they learned about their attendance and what changes they made as a result.

Leaders of Church 1 first noticed strong Easter attendance but soon realized how sporadic the attendance was both before and after Easter. They responded by planning a Lenten focus for the next year. They also utilized some of their special choirs more fully during Lent. They moved the reception of the confirmation class from Easter to the Sunday after Easter. Both worked well. In fact, the confirmands received more attention, and there was room for all their family members to sit together.

Leaders of Church 1 next noticed not only the summer slump, but also how long it lasted. This led to some rethinking of some of their summer assumptions. Instead of combining two services into one for the summer, the church continued both services and showed a 15 percent increase in summer attendance. Also, a major special focus was planned for the first Sunday after Labor Day to kick off the fall.

Church leaders were pleased to see the strong Advent and Christmas Eve attendance but realized that it took many weeks for strong attendance to return. The following year, they took the opportunity on Christmas Eve to promote a special January sermon series.

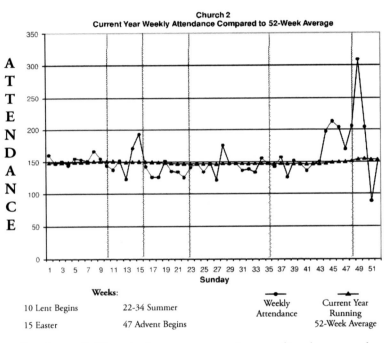

Church 2
Current Year Weekly Attendance Compared to 52-Week Average

Weeks:		
10 Lent Begins	22-34 Summer	Weekly Attendance
15 Easter	47 Advent Begins	Current Year Running 52-Week Average

Leaders of Church 2 were stunned to realize how modest their Easter attendance was compared to normal attendance and especially to a special Christmas musical presentation. Then they remembered that their one Easter service filled their space, and the Christmas musical attendance numbers represented many services held at different times. Because they normally have only one Sunday morning service, it had never occurred to them that Easter worship would not be at that time. The next year, they held two Easter services, used the new schedule as a reason to call everyone in the church to remind them of the new times, and doubled their Easter attendance. Like Church 1, they discovered the need for more effort both before and after Easter.

You will notice that Church 2 maintains its attendance in the summer far better than Church 1. The very high attendance Sunday during the summer is the week the church recognized "first responders" in the community such as police and firefighters. Notice also that there are two strong Sundays near the end of August and early in September. Because public schools begin in this community in early August, they have a back to school focus in August and then come back after Labor Day with a fall kick-off. And while they have a strong Christmas musical, they saw that not offering a Christmas Eve service was a missed opportunity.

We hope these examples help you anticipate the clues that can permit you to do what your church was established to do—help more people worship God and have the opportunity to hear the Gospel message. The chances that God will speak to someone through your church are far greater if they are in worship. Your careful attention to patterns and trends can bear much fruit for God.

CHAPTER 5

BIG DAYS

As we look at our worship on Easter and Christmas Eve, we learn that it is on these occasions when attendance surpasses the Sunday morning average in most of our congregations. Among the greatest opportunities for churches each year is what happens during Easter and Christmas Eve services. All year long, the church wonders what it can do to reach neighbors and friends to participate in the worship of God. Then, on two occasions in the Christian year, it is as if a homing beacon activates in less-attentive members, those who do not attend church, and those who are simply interested in what these Christian holidays mean. The number gathered for worship for these holy times may increase attendance dramatically.

To gather more information about attendance patterns, the Lewis Center administered a survey about worship attendance for these two special times. While this was not a scientific survey, it indicated that, on average, Easter attendance is 180 percent of the previous year's average worship attendance, ranging from just over 100 percent to 300 percent of average attendance. Christmas Eve attendance is, on average, 150 percent of the previous year's average worship attendance, ranging from just under 50 percent to over 300 percent. While all churches had Easter services, many reporting churches did not have Christmas Eve services.

Many members and visitors, it appears, will always come to worship on Easter and Christmas Eve—even if they do not attend at other times. But planning is still essential to ensure reaching current participants and connecting with new people. Planning is also critical as leaders explore how these services can be starting points for building attendance and thus reaching others in the period that follows these big attendance services. Church members need to be reminded of the centrality of these special times for Christians and the opportunity they provide to invite friends, family, and neighbors for whom they have been praying. A simple invitation to these persons they know well might begin, "If you do not have other plans for Easter (or Christmas Eve), we would be honored to have you join us for worship at our church."

WHAT WILL WE OFFER AT EASTER?

Easter is the high holy day for Christians. It is the celebration of the resurrection of Jesus Christ and the culmination of the message that, for Christians, death is not the last word. We remember the teachings of Jesus and recall the painful journey of his last days—and on this day, we sing a *new* song: *Jesus Christ is risen today!* Christ is risen not only from that tomb long ago. Christ is risen *today.* That is the glorious celebration of Easter worship. It is the time when faithful disciples rejoice and also seek to invite others to hear this amazing news of resurrection and new life.

Obviously, great attention should be given to every element of the worship experience. Easter is *the* special day of the Christian year, and the care and attention you give to it should reflect that fact. This does not mean that you should add so many extra parts that the service becomes longer than normal for your congregation. The focus should be on a worship experience fitting for Easter within the time you have.

Think about your church's attendance last Easter. Do you still have room to grow on Easter Sunday, given the location and schedule of how you are conducting worship on Easter? Or, do you need to consider changes in order to accommodate more worshipers on Easter? Think about your particular context as we consider what some possibilities are for building attendance. But remember, where you need to start depends on your situation.

Which one of these three descriptions best fits your church's attendance last Easter (not including sunrise services)?

1. We offered one service, and there was still room for more people.

2. We offered two services, and attendance filled or overflowed our space in at least one service.

3. We offered three or more services, and attendance was overflowing to the extent that people had to be seated in alternate locations for at least one of those services.

Scenario 1: We offered one service, and there was still room for more people.

If you still have room to grow within your existing worship configuration, then your task is to encourage more people to come to your service or services. Set a goal of surpassing last year's Easter attendance. Be bold in promoting it. Then, be sure to celebrate when it is accomplished.

This can begin with something as simple as reminding people of the importance of worship at this most holy time of year. Something is just not right if Christian people are not in church during Holy Week and on Easter. Churches can be frank and gracious at the same time. Building attendance out of guilt or obligation is not the goal. Talk about what people have experienced in Holy Week worship over the centuries and how much such worship can mean to their spiritual development.

If you have space for more people without adding another service, you have many options for building attendance—perhaps having multiple choirs sing. If, for example, your children's choirs are singing, parents and grandparents will want to attend. You can schedule confirmation or baptisms as a way of involving the friends and family of those being received.

Scenario 2: We offered two services, and attendance filled or overflowed our space in at least one service.

For all churches that offer more than one worship service regularly, there are several factors to keep in mind at Easter. Every Easter service should be of a quality to be an option for any person, no matter which service he or she regularly attends. Even if different worship services normally take on a distinctive character, make sure that every service offered for Easter is special.

Promote all of the services equally as your Easter services. Remember that people are not attending the "Saturday night service" or the "contemporary service" but "Easter worship." The services can be different, but all should reflect special planning for Easter so every service becomes an option for everyone.

What if space is tight in your existing Easter services? You can maximize your space on Easter and also have more attendance on other Sundays by considering options such as the following:

- Move confirmation to another Sunday, perhaps the Sunday after Easter or Pentecost, when the confirmands, their families, and this very significant time in their lives can receive more recognition.

- Instead of having multiple choirs sing on Easter, consider having them sing on Palm Sunday or other Sundays in Lent.

The next question to ask is whether an additional Sunday

morning worship service should be scheduled for Easter. The important question to consider is not "Do we have to do it?" but "Will an additional service make it more likely that we will reach more people through Easter worship than not having the extra service?" This may mean that the time of your normal service or services will need to be adjusted. Make sure there is widespread publicity about the times and that you are doing it to permit more people to experience Easter worship.

Scenario 3: We offered three or more services, and attendance was overflowing to the extent that people had to be seated in alternate locations in at least one service.

Some churches may have as many services as possible scheduled on Sunday morning and still not be able to accommodate more Easter worshipers. Although there are not many churches in this group, we can all glean ideas from ways they have addressed their desire to reach more people even when their space seems to be filled. Sometimes at this point in a church's development, leaders will choose to go to a large public building that will seat everyone.

Increasingly, churches that cannot offer more Sunday services are turning to adding an Easter service on Saturday night if they do not already have a Saturday evening service. At first, this idea seems strange. If people are not accustomed to worshiping on Saturday, then the idea of their Easter worship taking place on Saturday night seems not very attractive. In fact, just the opposite may be the case.

Some churches with many service times find that their Saturday evening service attendance is the highest on Easter weekend. That was Tom's experience the first time they tried a Saturday night Easter service to deal with lack of space prior to the building of their current larger sanctuary. In addition, their overall attendance jumped dramatically from the year before.

Because they could not add yet another service on Sunday morning, Saturday night became the time for the additional service. Tom personally did not think this was going to work. However, it turned out to be the most effective time that they could have offered. The most active members were asked to attend to make room for a visitor on Sunday morning. Many reported how much they appreciated the service time. This service resolved many family dilemmas around competing claims on Easter Sunday. Some chose to worship on Sunday with family in other churches in addition to worshiping at their own church. Adding this extra service, even at an unfamiliar time for the congregation, meant that more people by far were reached for Easter worship than would have been possible without the service.

After a few years of adding Easter celebrations on Saturday night, the church Tom serves built a new sanctuary that provided ample space for Easter worship. However, the church leadership knew that something would be lost if they no longer offered the service on Saturday evening. Rather than hold the same service that they would have on Sunday, the Saturday service became an opportunity for baptism, including baptism by immersion. The church did not have a baptismal tank but was able to borrow a portable baptismal for this purpose. While this required some extra planning, there were adults in the congregation who decided to be baptized because the occasion was linked to Easter and the baptism was offered by immersion. They were able to invite family and friends to the Saturday evening service, knowing that those who were Christians might be attending their own churches on Sunday morning. They were also able to invite friends who had no church home as well. Even if your church is a long way from needing to add services because of space limitations, examples from other churches may spark your own "out of the box" ideas that fit your situation.

And here is a new way to think about the use of overflow worship space. Often, when overflow space is needed, it is the visitors who are placed there, because they may be the last ones to arrive. This is not the best way to ensure your visitors feel welcome and have a quality worship experience. If you need to use overflow space, make sure that the people seated there are not visitors, but regular worshipers.

Handling overflow seating well is difficult but very important. You start with the disadvantage that no matter what you provide for overflow seating, it is not the preferable seating people expected in the main worship area. Everyone would rather be in the sanctuary. Ensuring that overflow space is used by regular worshipers instead of visitors helps if you can achieve this goal. One way to do so is to ask members to "own" certain overflow spaces. Some Sunday school classes and other small groups can be asked through their leader, "You have twelve people in your small group. Could you ask them and their families to 'take over' one of the overflow spaces for Easter (or for Christmas Eve)?" One good feature about this arrangement in Tom's experience is that when the people in that overflow space know each other, they enjoy the camaraderie, sing better, and do not complain as much about not being in the sanctuary. The whole experience becomes more meaningful for them, and they have the satisfaction of knowing they are contributing in an important way to the church's mission to reach others for Christ.

And for all churches—no matter what your past attendance has been—as you look toward Easter, assume you are going to have more people than you have ever had and make plans accordingly.

WHAT WILL WE OFFER AT CHRISTMAS EVE?

Churches without Christmas Eve services may be missing a "53rd Sunday" when many churches show attendance rivaling Easter. And churches with low attendance at Christmas Eve services may want to explore how to enhance their offerings to reach more people. In formulating plans to increase attendance at Christmas Eve, you may want to consider the following ideas.

What do other churches in your surrounding area do for Christmas Eve in terms of number of services, timing of services, and so on? Survey carefully. While it can be helpful to offer something distinctive on Christmas Eve, keep in mind that there are certain experiences most people are looking for that night: good music, a relevant message, and candlelight.

No matter what size the church, find at least one fine solo or choral piece that will be shared that night. Pastors and worship leaders should work with musicians in the musical selection process for Christmas Eve and work far enough in advance that the choir or soloists have adequate time to prepare their music. Meeting together permits sharing hopes for how the music and message will enable those who do not worship often to enter into the sacred space of worship and draw closer to Christ.

Pray with your music leaders, and ask God to bless their efforts. There are few occasions when the music is more likely to communicate the total message of a special celebration in the life of the church than Christmas Eve. If you do not have a gifted soloist or full choir, consider asking someone from outside your congregation to share his or her talents that night. Vocalists are often looking for an opportunity to share their gifts, especially on occasions like Christmas Eve or Easter. Such an opportunity may be something your members will want to share with those they are inviting to worship. Christmas Eve is a night when church members should look forward to a very special time of worship just as they look forward to something special at their meals and social gatherings. This holy time is a gift to offer to God and will help draw people into a more sacred and joyful time of worship.

It will be important that the sermon for Christmas Eve is a clear proclamation of the gospel that is engaging and only as long as it needs to be to communicate the love of God demonstrated in the incarnation. It is not that the sermon needs to be short, as much as it needs to be memorable and compelling to any guests who join you that night. It should be prepared more with visitors in mind than members and should therefore be a more basic communication of the Christian message. The birth of Christ is that old, old story that we can hear annually and yet still find fresh each year. And it can be that inviting message of good news that will touch someone who has never truly heard the message of grace and hope.

In your website or phone message communication, you can tell people that at the conclusion of the service, they will be able to join in lighting a candle and singing "Silent Night," if this is the custom of your congregation. People often associate these traditions with a Christmas Eve service. If they have moved to the area and are looking for a place to worship, it may be the significant information that will lead them to join you. When people call churches to inquire about these services, one of the most common questions asked is "Will we light a candle at the end?" Many people in your community understand, before the sermon is ever preached, that the world can be a very painful place and that God's love is a light in the midst of struggle. From the stars that were followed by shepherds and magi, to the theological imagery in John 1, light is a central image associated with the story of the incarnation. It also provides the pastor with a rich opportunity to interpret the ways the church provides hope and love in the community for guests less familiar with its ministry.

Other elements to be included in your Christmas Eve planning: Consider giving a modest gift to all your Christmas Eve visitors, such as a Christmas ornament or homemade Christmas cookies. Remember that people are likely to attend Christmas Eve services as a family, so it will be important that your service have elements especially prepared for small children.

Do not be afraid to take an offering for fear it will "turn off" nonchurch people. The key is to make sure it is an offering for others. People like to see that the church is reaching beyond itself. Church leaders are wise to consider ways to give away the entire Christmas Eve offering to a ministry the church supports. If the congregation supports a local free medical clinic, for example, and the Christmas Eve offering is designated for this purpose, the church will probably be able to give more than it planned to give only by taking a special offering on a regular Sunday or by including it in the budget. There are at least three reasons why your church wants to give away the Christmas Eve offering: excitement among your members, the testimony you create among your guests, and the significant response of infrequent worshipers.

Excitement among Your Members

When the church leadership states that the entire Christmas Eve offering is to be given away to one or two worthy places of ministry, it creates a sense of vitality in the congregation. Many long-term members know the ministry of their church so well that there are few moments of anticipation or surprise left. They know the annual cycles of the liturgical calendar and administration of the church. Like a marriage that can grow stale due to unaltered routine, these members benefit when their church does something surprising, like extravagant generosity at Christmas.

Some church leaders may be concerned that people will replace their regular offering, which supports the life of the congregation, with a special offering on Christmas Eve. This was certainly the concern when the church Tom serves made the decision to follow the lead of other congregations who gave away this offering. What surprised everyone was that members became more likely to fulfill their pledge to the church because they knew that if the Christmas Eve offering was being given away, members would need to be fully reliable in their giving. The reason that people gave to both is that most people found that they had a separate "pocket" for money they gave away on Christmas Eve in addition to the one they used to give to the church for its annual budget.

The joy of giving these funds with their church family enabled them to feel better about their church than they had in a long time, which motivated their giving in the coming year. Giving away this offering created a sense of excitement, as church members reported that before they opened their Christmas gifts with friends or family, they looked on the church website to see what the congregation had given to those in need through the offering. This was the first gift of Christmas, fitting for the Christ whose ministry leads followers to care for those who are poor or in need.

Testimony among Guests

Guests leave Christmas Eve services having experienced a testimony of generosity by the church. Be aware that many guests on Christmas Eve come with a cynical frame of mind. They have been brought there by family or friends and may even feel a bit coerced in the process. The usual claims may be running through their minds as they sit in the pew: *all they care about is the offering; nothing authentic happening here.*

Once it is made clear that not a dollar will benefit the church and they are invited to join in the generosity of the congregation and hear how others will be blessed, it is hard for them to hold harsh opinions of the church. Suddenly the conversation they share over Christmas dinner or in the community the following week is very different. If they can see the results of the offering later, such as an update on the church website or some other communication, they will have something to share with their friends who also may not attend a church.

85

We are in a time when the church does not have a very good reputation among many people who do not attend church. There is no better communication about the church than the positive comments of those who do not regularly attend, especially if they have been known to be cynical about religion in general and Christianity in particular. One woman in Tom's congregation shared that her uncle, who described himself as very distant from God, was amazed by the offering and was joyful when he heard the total amount given on Christmas Eve. This opened up a conversation between this man and his niece in which she was able to share her faith in a deeper way to a much more receptive uncle than she had encountered in years past. She was grateful that her church opened this door to a deeper relationship with her uncle, whose diminished cynicism made him a far more intrigued listener.

Significant Response among Infrequent Worshipers

There are two groups that any church is hoping will attend the church more frequently who are likely to be present on Christmas Eve. The first are guests. The second are long-term members who attend only at Christmas and Easter. Both are served well by this unusual moment of generosity. Guests will be appreciative of the consistency of the church that lives out what God has modeled in the incarnation. God comes to us in our time of need. The church gives its offering to others in their time of need. Members who attend infrequently may have a renewed sense that a fresh wind of the Spirit is blowing through their church. If they have been disappointed by the church for some reason in the past, the experience of the offering and the way the church is involved in the community or world may provide a reason to return.

One final word about Christmas Eve is that your church may have many members who are out of town on Christmas Eve.

Some churches regularly schedule a Travelers' Christmas Eve Service at a time prior to Christmas Eve to permit those who will be traveling or any others for whom a different date works best to celebrate Christmas Eve worship at their church.[1]

WHOM WILL WE INVITE AT EASTER AND CHRISTMAS EVE, AND HOW?

Given the importance of Easter and Christmas Eve—not only in terms of our faith journey but also in terms of its potential for reaching more worshipers with the message of the resurrection and the birth of Christ—we need to go beyond what is normally done to extend an invitation.

In addition to current members, some others to consider include the following:

- recent visitors

- friends and family of members

- persons connected with some ministry of your church, for example, families of children enrolled in a preschool or scout troop

- people in the immediate vicinity of your church

- persons without a church home

- others?

First, in terms of your current members, find a reason for every household to be called the week before these special days. It could be a reminder that there will be an extra service or that the service times will be a bit different or just "we are calling every home to wish you a blessed Holy Week (or Christmas) and to remind you that special Easter (Christmas Eve) worship is planned." Easter and Christmas Eve also give opportunities to call all those who have visited in the past six months or so.

You will also want to reach out to those in your community who have not yet attended your church. As you think about options, weigh your resources and the benefits of each to decide what actions make the most sense for you. Everything needs to be judged based on how likely it is to increase the number of people you reach with the special messages of worship on Easter or Christmas Eve.

Direct mail and social media are significant options. Determine the geographic area you want to reach as precisely as possible and then design and send an appealing direct mail piece. Find examples of what other churches have done. The same is true for other forms of publicizing. Provide copies of the direct mail piece to your members to give to their friends. Most publishers who provide direct mail pieces will also supply an electronic version. This can be a valuable tool for churches to provide to members so that they can send personal invitations to their friends through e-mail or social media. Asking members to invite their friends and then providing them the means will make it much more likely that they will follow through. During the prayer time in worship during Advent, ask people to write down names of people they think would be blessed by the experience of Christmas Eve worship. Give them a time of silence to pray for these persons during worship and then ask them to call or send an invitation to those on their list. If the church provides a written or electronic invitation, it can serve as a great follow-up to their verbal invitation or can be a suitable invitation for their acquaintances.

Social media provides expanding channels to invite others both through the church's presence and, perhaps more productively, by giving members tools they can use to share with their social media friends. A short video clip or well-designed invitation can give them the occasion to invite others seeking a place to worship, as suggested above. Also engage your social media and that of your members to alert people to extra worship services or special details about the Easter or Christmas Eve services that might help people decide to come or which service to attend.

Consider more creative and interactive ways of reaching out to your community. For example, go to a park or playground and give people bottles of water with the church's name and an invitation to worship; this is an example of "servant evangelism." One church that sits on a highly traveled street placed an attractive banner in front of the church with the message "You Are Invited to Candlelight Christmas Eve Worship," along with the service time. Attendance increased from 80 to 300 that year.

Whatever you do, make sure it is done well. It is far better to do fewer promotional things that can be done well and thoroughly than to scatter energy and resources in too many directions. Begin somewhere and add avenues of outreach each year.

HOW WILL WE WELCOME THEM?

Leaders and all members need to be prepared and coached to receive guests as the "hosts of Christ" that all of us are called to be. Keep in mind that people are present at Easter and Christmas Eve who are not regular churchgoers. As you plan, review everything from their perspective. Imagine dear loved ones who are coming to church for the first time since childhood. Will what is said and done make sense to them? Will the spirit and movement and content of the service make such a person feel welcome and want to return? Simple is better than complex. Remove unnecessary stumbling blocks for those new to church. Provide written or spoken instructions where newcomers most need them. The preferences and plans of those closest to worship must always be viewed through the eyes of those you seek to reach.

Assume you are going to have more people than you have ever had and make plans accordingly. Put the same care into preparing for these guests that you would devote to making plans for guests coming to your home. Some aspects to make sure are ready to accommodate members and guests include the following:

- greeters and ushers at every entrance used by members or guests

- nursery

- parking attendants and greeters

- reserved parking for guests

- restrooms

- entry areas

- signage—external and internal

Will attention to every detail make persons know you are a community of faith that welcomes them—from the moment they approach the church until they leave following the service of worship? Churches sometimes have to use classrooms and other spaces for overflow seating areas for special services through videocast. Make sure these areas have something special that is not available in the main seating space. The church Tom serves had to use classrooms on Christmas Eve until a sanctuary was built. Coffee was purchased from a local coffee shop and light refreshments were added as well. This created a more inviting atmosphere and gave people a reason to gather in the hallway prior to the service where they could greet each other before moving into the smaller rooms for the service. Make sure to welcome those in the classrooms when the service begins. After the benediction, if pastors can make their way to the overflow seating area to greet those who worshiped there, it will go a long way toward making them feel more welcomed and appreciated.

HOW WILL WE FOLLOW UP?

After the worship experiences of these "big days," the important question church leaders must ask is how to build upon these opportunities with a plan to welcome these visitors back to worship regularly.

First, follow up with all Easter and Christmas Eve visitors in a timely manner. Do not let the exhaustion of Easter and Christmas preparations get in the way of a prompt response. Keep in mind that you will have many more visitors than usual so you will need to have in place the extra people to do the follow-up that will need to be done. Do not count on your normal systems being sufficient for this task.

Your follow-up will be made much easier if a compelling sermon series or other special emphasis is announced to begin after Easter or in January. Make it as easy as possible for newcomers to return and to become involved quickly while their interest is high. Such options as an information booth or table, sign-up tables for upcoming programs, and literature about an upcoming sermon series make it more likely that people will return.

You have heard it said that "you have only one chance to make a first impression." Remember that you have only one chance a year to make an "Easter impression" or a "Christmas Eve impression." Sharing the stories of the birth and resurrection of Christ should prompt a caring follow-up so people know you are welcoming them into the community of faith.

CHAPTER 6

PRIME SEASONS

Prime seasons are the times of the year when people are more likely to attend worship in higher numbers than at any other times except the two "big days" of Christmas Eve and Easter. Some seasons are "prime" because they are traditionally significant in the calendar of the Christian year. Others reflect times of the year when the whole community is likely to be focused on special events or transitions.

ADVENT

Advent is a prime season with rich potential for engaging church members and new people. There is arguably no time in the year when people are more interested in what the church is offering than during Advent. The music of the church continues to be a major portion of the music of the surrounding culture during December. What attracts many to church this time of year is the realization that the church shares this season in a way that has greater meaning and integrity than their local shopping mall or holiday show in the theater. Whether with a gathering of neighbors singing carols in a small country church, or with a large choir and organ in a tall steeple sanctuary, the church understands how to celebrate Advent and Christmas.

There are many themes that can be explored during Advent that reinforce these weeks as a time of spiritual preparation for the coming of the Messiah in Bethlehem and the second coming of the Christ. With words like hope, forgiveness, repentance, promise, and covenant, along with the words of the prophets and the stories of Mary, Joseph, and the angels that greeted them, preachers will have no problem finding relevant topics for sermons. The lectionary serves the preacher well during the Advent and Christmas cycle, inviting the congregation to see the connections between the Old and New Testaments and the announcement of the Christ child.

This is a time of year to consider the experiences and activities that support worship. December is a time when people are looking for experiences to share with friends and families. Church leaders can plan in advance to offer events and guide individuals and families in ways that will bring greater meaning to Christmas preparations.

First, consider the full experience of Advent. Some of the most important worship that will take place will be in the personal devotional space that people create this time of year. Because of the pace of December, with its special decorations, parties, gifts, and other activities that people enjoy, they may be less likely to make time for personal devotion. It is the role of the church to empower the spiritual focus of Advent.

Barbara, the associate pastor at the church Tom serves, asked a group of church members to talk in September about Advent and Christmas and share what the church could do to make the season more meaningful. One of the participants, Bill, shared that his family had a tradition of making an Advent log. The Advent log was essentially a traditional Advent wreath that used a log with five holes drilled into it for the candles. Bill shared how he and his father would prepare the log, stapling fresh greenery to its sides, and he described the joy of lighting the candles as the family shared daily devotions.

Tom realized that Bill's father had taken an Advent wreath and combined three elements that no boy could resist: wood, power tools, and fire. Building on this idea, a group of men in the church was organized to gather logs, pre-drill the holes, cut greens, and invite the congregation to come prepare Advent logs. Advent candles and devotional booklets were provided. Over one hundred families and individuals gathered to make their own Advent logs. The congregation was challenged to set apart time each day to light the Advent candles and share a daily devotion. The worship we encourage should be beyond the sanctuary, in the homes and private spaces of the lives of our church members.

During the meeting with church members, another theme became clear: music. People said that while they appreciated sermons throughout the year, the message of Advent and Christmas was often best conveyed in song. They shared that some of their best memories of the season were found in singing at local community events. While they loved the hymns of the church, they wished that Advent could include a service of singing similar to what they found at the "Christmas sing-a-long" at the nearby park amphitheater.

Some pastors find it inappropriate to sing Christmas carols during Advent. The tradition of the church is to sing songs that reflect Advent as a time of preparation, and not break into the celebration of Christ's birth before the time. The problem with this thinking is that the surrounding culture of the United States does not follow the lead of the church, and this culture now leads the way for the experience of the season. Radio stations in most major markets now start playing non-stop Christmas music not after Thanksgiving, as they did in past years, but after Halloween! Churches that refuse to sing Christmas carols until December 24 are in danger of being the only venue where such music is not sung during December. The church, therefore, becomes a place people may avoid, since the experience of hearing and singing this music is offered abundantly elsewhere. What is lost is the sacred nature of the music. When choirs appear at the local mall, they mix "Joy to the World" with "Rudolph the Red-Nosed Reindeer." Soon, the message of the sacred is so blended with the secular that it has no power and certainly no significance for worship.

Hearing this desire to sing the music of the season, the leaders of the weekly 5:00 p.m. service in the church Tom serves reformatted worship for the first week of Advent as a time to sing the carols of the season. This service was held immediately following the completion of the Advent log event. The usual worship attendance of 150 swelled to over 500 persons as the sanctuary filled with joyful music.

Bill, who had shared the Advent log tradition months earlier, came forward with his wife, Jessica, and their children and demonstrated how an Advent devotion was shared in their home. Because many in the church had never participated in such a tradition, it was important to model this for the congregation. The church did not use its traditional Advent wreath that year, choosing instead to have a larger version of the Advent log in the front of the sanctuary as a way of communicating that everyone in the church was on the same journey during Advent. This service was followed by a soup supper, where members of the church had time to share a simple meal and catch up with one another as their Advent season began. It was enjoyable to see members of the church linger around the tables, enjoying their conversation, meeting new friends, and visiting with each other.

Worship in Advent can also be an act of pastoral care. The season brings many memories and expectations of happiness that can be difficult for those who have lost loved ones in the past year or who are facing personal challenges of illness, unemployment, or mental health issues such as depression. Many churches offer a "Darkness to Light" service, focused on the promised hope of the Messiah and the presence of the incarnate love of God in the world and in our lives. This service is often held a few days before Christmas, on the winter solstice, and may be called a "Longest Night" service.

It is important that the introduction and invitation to this service not dwell on issues of grief, depression, or sadness, even if the intent is to offer a sense of hope to people experiencing these emotions. A church member once approached Tom and asked, "When is the sad people service?" That is when Tom knew a new announcement for the service needed to be crafted. One aspect of this service that people find meaningful is that it can provide more times of silence and reflection. The new announcement emphasized the service as a time of quiet and contemplation, with experiential elements such as Holy Communion, votive candles for intercession, and opportunities for prayer. Worship stations at the end of this service provide these opportunities and include laypersons and clergy who pray individually with those who attend so that they can share where in their lives they need to experience hope and healing. The pace of this time can move slowly and have less emphasis on preaching, but more time for prayer and singing. Many songs written for Advent that reflect a sense of longing for God are especially meaningful for this service. The goal of this additional service during Advent is to partner worship with pastoral care and allow people to enter the presence of God to experience comfort and healing.

Another aspect of this season is to assist the congregation in their desire to bless others, especially those who are in situations of poverty. Many community organizations and non-profits can use help during the Christmas season. A shelter for abused women, for example, may benefit from gift cards for women who are there with their children prior to Christmas without any gifts for Christmas Day. The homeless shelter may want hats and gloves or other items. Organizations from the Salvation Army to Toys for Tots are grateful when churches ask how they can assist the good work they are doing. These collections benefit the members of the church who want to teach their children to give to others and who see Christmas as a time to follow the example of the Magi, bringing gifts to the Christ child. People are excited to attend a church that is generous and outwardly focused. When

97

churches build off these experiences to develop ongoing, year-long relationships with these organizations and those they serve, they can begin to do serious work in transforming people's lives in their community.

LENT

The Lenten season is another prime season. The weeks between Ash Wednesday and Easter hold many possibilities, especially with current members. They may be more open to participating in a class, reading a book tied to a sermon series, or committing to attendance and other goals because it is Lent.

Lent is a time for going more deeply into Christian discipleship. The good news is that this focus is in no way counter-productive to the goal of reaching out to others and increasing worship attendance. Church members are often aware that Lent is a season for increased devotion to Christ that lends itself to study, prayer, and introspection. This is an ideal time to call the congregation to a deepening of their discipleship over the six weeks of Lent and to find ways to make these weeks welcoming to those who might be new to the church.

One of the ways that Tom challenged his congregation to participate in worship and study during Lent was to take up "The Lent Challenge." Tom acknowledged that many gave something up for Lent, often an item like chocolate or dessert. While calories were fewer for the faithful, such discipline did little to transform lives. Besides, "giving up" these things often left people dour and cranky, gateways into sins other than gluttony. Instead of "giving up" sweets, church members were called to "take up" the daily reading of scripture, involvement in a weekly small group, and participation in weekly worship. By infusing their lives with the reading of the Bible, Christian conversation, and six consecutive weeks of worship, they could truly honor Christ and seek a deeper faith experience during Lent.

98

Months earlier, Tom had worked with a layperson in the congregation to develop a video series entitled *Six Things Everybody Ought to Know about God*. You can see this curriculum at www.6blocks.com. The curriculum included a participant's guide, leader's guide, and weekly videos to help facilitate the small group experience. The congregation was invited to sign up for small groups, and leaders were trained. Many who joined these groups had never participated in the past. The defined time period and challenge motivated them to give this a try. The experience also brought a greater sense of unity as members were reading the same material, participating in similar small group conversations, and hearing a sermon each week that focused on the topic of the week.

While the sermon series was important, it was the encouragement to participate in the daily workbook and the weekly small groups that led to deepening discipleship and increased worship attendance. Having everyone on the same journey made a big difference in the experience of Lent. Momentum builds over the weeks of the sermon series as people work to complete the study together, both encouraging one another and holding one another accountable as the weeks pass. You do not have to write your own curriculum to make this experience possible. Many books and small group materials are available for study and devotional reading during the six weeks of Lent.

It is important to conclude Lent with a meaningful Holy Week. Holy Thursday and Good Friday are critical worship experiences because of their theological focus on the significance of Holy Communion and the meaning of the events of Good Friday. People of faith miss crucial dimensions of the Gospel message when they jump from Palm Sunday into Easter, avoiding the pain and sorrow of the arrest, suffering, and crucifixion of Christ. Christians need to experience the full range of Christ's saving work represented in the journey of Holy Week.

Again, many Christians know that it is appropriate for the

99

pastor to call them to deeper devotion during Lent. Tom even chose confrontation one year when he announced:

> This is the week when we remember that our Lord gave his life for the forgiveness of our sins. Yet many Christians do not attend either Holy Thursday or Good Friday services. I challenge you to consider that if you are eating a late dinner on Thursday and miss the opportunity to commune with Christ, something is out of place in your life. If you are home watching television or out with friends on Friday as we gather at the foot of our Savior's cross, something is wrong with your faith. Come walk with Jesus this week. Give these hours to prayer and worship and honor the Son of God who has given his life for us.

Tom's intention was not to heap guilt on the congregation but to speak candidly about the purpose of these services and how appropriate it was to prioritize our time so that we could gather as a church for worship. This was a part of "The Lent Challenge," and attendance increased significantly for these Holy Week services. More importantly, many reported later that they had a new experience of God's love and grace as a result of the services. They were able to commune with Christ in a meaningful way on Thursday. They sought the grace and forgiveness of Christ when they contemplated his crucifixion, and they had a renewed awareness of God's love for the world, as symbolized in the cross that was given to them on Good Friday.

The weeks of Lent and services of Holy Week are an excellent time for outstanding music. Many churches are discovering that the key to music in the current environment is not connected to style as much as quality. If the music is done poorly, it does not matter if it is a grand organ or an electric guitar. Likewise, if the music that is played and sung is excellent, people are often able to hear a style they might not normally select and will experience evocative worship. Churches that offer multiple styles of worship are wise to vary the style during Holy Week services so that everyone's choice is honored. The music is important because the beauty of the words, voices, and instruments often speak to the deep places of the heart that even an excellent sermon is not likely to reach.

Leaders who plan worship can enlist the help of talented vocalists and musicians who may not be a part of the church, but who are available through local colleges or choral guilds. Tom once invited a student from a local music conservatory to sing in a very small country church. His specialty was classical music and opera. Everyone was fairly certain that his selections had never been sung at that church in its one hundred-plus-year history. While Fanny Crosby and Hank Williams had long been accepted there, Bach and Handel had rarely appeared. And no one could remember anyone ever singing in Latin. Despite the diversion from the status quo, the beauty of the music moved the congregation. They were very appreciative of the obvious level of preparation the young man had given to the music he shared, and they expressed their joy at the talent God had given him. As one elderly woman put it, "I don't know what he said, but it sounded like an angel. I hope heaven is full of that music." While the student certainly experienced other grateful audiences later in his life, it is doubtful that any surpassed the unlikely gratitude of that small congregation.

Another congregation hosted the local community choir, which was made up of members of various churches and people in the community who enjoyed singing but had no church home. The church invited them to use their sanctuary for weekly rehearsal. In return, the choir paid to have the piano tuned regularly and held two concerts a year that filled the sanctuary. When one of these concerts was moved to Holy Week, the pastor was able to add scripture and prayer and make it a Good Friday service that would have been hard to establish in his small church. Such opportunities are available for those who seek them.

If worship leaders are not sure where to find such musicians, a quick Internet search will often reveal individuals and groups who are willing to sing in churches for little or no compensation. The key is to make sure there is some way to hear a sample of the music before the invitation is issued. Many websites offer excerpts of past concerts or music that can be downloaded for a modest fee. It is well worth the time and effort to find a way to informally audition the person or group to make sure that the experience will be a good one for the congregation.

A cantata or similar choral arrangement can be offered on a Sunday in Lent or during Holy Week. If pastors and music leaders work together to craft the music into a service of worship that includes scripture, prayer, and even a brief message rather than simply offering a concert, a dramatic increase in attendance may occur. Members of the church are far more likely to invite their friends to a service when they know it will feature music that is both meaningful and excellent. If the music they are sharing is well known, it can easily be advertised in the community and through the congregation's social media outlets. There are people in your community who are looking for places where the music they appreciate is shared. Once they realize that this is a part of the life of your congregation, they may choose to make it their church home.

JANUARY/FEBRUARY

It is important to move into the new calendar year with energy and enthusiasm. Emphasize the new year as a time for new beginnings and spiritual resolutions.

January is the perfect time to offer a sermon series that will attract Christmas Eve visitors or inactive members. The sermon series, as well as any supporting small groups or programs, can be announced Christmas Eve with a warm invitation to return for the upcoming series. Topics for this series should be important to those the church is seeking to reach. One way to discover what a helpful series might be is to reach out to the congregation with a survey in the bulletin or through social media. Ask participants to choose the top three series from five or six options and then leave room for any ideas they would like to offer. January is a time when people are thinking about resolutions for change in the coming year. Sermon series that talk about transformation of habits, relationships, finances, or health will often resonate with this desire for a new experience in a new year. Likewise, series that show people new ways to relate to God through spiritual practices will assist the congregation in its discipleship. The key is to be prepared with not only a series, but also a book, small group experience, or workshop that might accompany the Sunday worship experience.

FALL AND BACK TO SCHOOL

The post-summer season when vacations tend to end and school resumes is another prime season. This is an excellent time to focus on children and their return to schools in the community and the beginning of the new Sunday school year. When school begins is typically the beginning of the church's programming year. Take time to pray for students. Younger children can be encouraged to participate in a "blessing of the backpacks" in worship where they are invited to come forward for a time of prayer for the coming school year. The pastor can speak to the importance of learning and the ways they can honor their new teachers. Teachers from many settings can be invited to attend this service as well—teachers from the church's preschool, local schools, and Sunday school, and parents who homeschool their children. These teachers can be given a pin or other identification as they enter the sanctuary so that they can be recognized and thanked. A special time of prayer during the service for these servants, along with a time of acknowledgment, is a way to appreciate the role of teachers and create a special invitation.

If the church has a relationship with a local school, it can invite the faculty to attend. A service component can be added if the church is asked to bring backpacks or school supplies for children in need in the community. Such an activity increases the likelihood that people will attend that Sunday and provides those attending the church with a sense that their congregation cares about children in the local community beyond the walls of the church.

The new Sunday school year also offers opportunities. These may include Promotion Day, presentation of Bibles, and dedication of church school teachers. Including such recognitions as an integral part of worship lifts up the connection between worship and study and gives attention to people not often involved in worship leadership.

Holding a Sunday School Rally Day the Sunday after Labor Day is not a worship activity, but it will encourage worship attendance. Such a Sunday gives the occasion to invite everyone to join a class and for all existing classes to reach out to their members and prospective members. It also makes a wonderful marker for the start of the new Sunday school year.

Many churches also have a Fall Kick-off Sunday to begin the new season of church programming. Often there is a theme that is reflected in the programming to come and perhaps is included in a sermon series and the worship elements. One church located where schools begin in August had a major Sunday built around children and school in August and then a Fall Kick-off in September.

THE SERMON SERIES AS AN OUTREACH OPPORTUNITY IN PRIME SEASONS

A sermon series, as described in Chapter 3, can be of great assistance in the effort to reach new disciples as well as deepen the faith of current members during these prime times. As we have pointed out, members may feel comfortable sharing a simple invitation with a friend to come and participate in a sermon series through which a friend might be nourished and know healing.

Another benefit of a sermon series is that it may provide those who are new to the congregation a reason to persist in attendance through the duration of the series. This enables them to meet members of the church, hear announcements that invite them to participate in other aspects of the church's life, and find their place in God's sanctuary. A series invites the congregation to take a journey together, to consider a topic that is common to the human experience in light of the wisdom of the Bible. It enables people to feel that over the course of weeks, God is speaking to them about something important. A series can be even more helpful to those new to the congregation if it includes the opportunity to join a small group or be involved in another activity related to the series. When church becomes relevant to people, they will attend worship weekly for fear of missing something important if they are not present.

MAKING THE MOST OF ATTENDANCE SEASONS

There are many "seasons" to which church leaders need to give attention. While the liturgical year shapes the content of worship as it reminds worshipers of God's mighty work through Jesus Christ, there are those other seasons (program, school, weather) that will guide how plans are implemented. Likewise, your attendance seasons will give you clues for the most appropriate planning needed to ensure that your church is reaching the most people for the worship of God across the span of the entire year. Two of these seasons, Advent and Lent, especially lend themselves to strengthening involvement by current constituents, while the beginning of the calendar year and the beginning of the school year present ideal opportunities to reach new people as well as current members. In every season, however, attentive leaders look for clues to guide the faithful and fruitful planning that will bring the Gospel to those still outside the church and will deepen the discipleship of those who are already committed to living the Good News.

LOW TIMES

The time after Easter and the summer months are, in most churches, times of diminished worship attendance. Many churches have been attentive to this challenge and have made special plans for their worship during these times.

POST-EASTER

Churches that offer confirmation classes for students know that the worship service that culminates the experience is often well attended by parents, family members, and friends who come to mark the occasion as a rite of passage. Confirmation is a process in which participants study the foundational doctrine and theology of the church, become familiar with spiritual disciplines, and spend time considering creeds and the tradition of the church. It can be as short as three months or as long as two years, depending on the church tradition. At the end of confirmation, students are invited to participate in Christian baptism, if they were not baptized at a younger age, and take vows of membership. Confirmation is a special event because it is the individual's first public affirmation of faith in Christ.

The early church often culminated an extended period of teaching for new converts at Easter. The day designated to celebrate the resurrection of Christ was an especially appropriate time to celebrate the new life in Christ converts expressed as they were baptized and received into the fellowship of the church. Many churches place Easter and confirmation Sunday together as a result. There are benefits to reconsidering this practice related to Easter. If it is important to associate confirmation Sunday with the resurrection, it can be held at any point in the Easter season, which includes the seven Sundays following Easter.

The Sunday after Easter is often the lowest-attended Sunday in the year, on par with the Sunday after Christmas, and has all the bounce of a deflated balloon. Only seven days have passed since the great celebration, but beyond a smaller group of faithful attenders, the church has often lost even the triumphal echoes of Easter morning. Moving confirmation Sunday to this week following Easter brings the families and friends of the students to the church and reminds the congregation that the resurrection is not a single celebration. The decision to be confirmed reinforces the theme of new life and resurrection but is not overshadowed in the traditions of the service on Easter Sunday.

Celebrating confirmation on the Sunday after Easter has the added benefit of helping some who might otherwise come to worship only on Easter to attend two weeks in a row. Learning to attend worship with consistency is difficult for many. Part of what is necessary is to convince such persons that they can conform the habits of their lives to come to church more than once a year or once a month. By following Easter with confirmation, the church is helping these persons build the muscles of a good habit, and they may be more likely to attend in the weeks following.

The confirmation service is a great opportunity to continue for a second week in a row the high quality found in most Easter services. Special music and attention to the way in which students are confirmed can make a significant difference. This service is special and should have a focus on the decision those being confirmed are making to commit their lives to Christ. One church looked at the way pastors were ordained in their denomination and modeled the act of confirmation accordingly. The pastor's sermon was a personal address to the confirmation students that the rest of the congregation overheard. It included an illustration in which two of the students participated in a simple object lesson taken from a science textbook that engaged the confirmands. When the time came for the confirmation, rather than bringing the whole class as a large group, each student came forward to a kneeler. Parents and the confirmation mentors stood behind the kneeling students and placed their hands on the students' shoulders while the pastor confirmed them in the faith. A volunteer photographer was present to capture the moment discreetly and avoid turning the event into a press conference by friends and family. These pictures were then given as a gift to the confirmation students to mark this important event.

The church found that taking time in the service to make the act of confirmation more significant encouraged more to attend that service of worship the following years. Parents knew that the Sunday would be special for their children and invited more guests to attend and celebrate this important rite of passage. It is important not to use something as sacred as confirmation as a device to boost worship attendance. The point made here is that, after careful consideration of how the service is best done and when it is more likely to stand out in the life of the congregation, more people gathered for worship, including some the church may not have reached before. A Sunday that was the lowest of the year became the third highest in attendance.

Considering the significance of other Sundays on the liturgical calendar can also be valuable. Pentecost is the Sunday that marks the day when the Holy Spirit fell on Peter and the other disciples and led to the birth of the church. One congregation decided Pentecost would be an excellent time for its members to remember their baptismal covenant and rededicate themselves as disciples of Jesus Christ. They celebrated Holy Communion and provided an opportunity for members to be anointed with oil and place their hands in the baptismal font as a way to remember and reaffirm the vows of their baptism. Prior to this service, the pastor sent everyone a letter that encouraged their participation and explained the symbolism of the various opportunities the service presented. A group of men built a fountain in front of the church for that Sunday, a strong visual reminder of water that told everyone entering that something special was happening that day.

Another church found a way to reach more people over the Memorial Day weekend. Instead of focusing on those who tend to be gone over three-day holiday weekends, they identified those who tend not to travel over such holidays. They discovered that it is their older members who are in town. So they planned a special recognition event for long-time members, and it attracted many of their family and friends who were able to visit over the holiday. With so many newer members joining the church, there was a need to remember the loyalty of older members, and Memorial Day proved to be an ideal time for something they had needed to do for a long time. Imagine the ancillary benefits to this event. After the church service, a picnic could be held when church members could reacquaint themselves with one another. Games might be played where people would interact, learn each other's names, and create a memory together. Older members could be invited to share special memories of the church that would allow newer members to enter into the church's larger story. The fellowship of this recognition Sunday would contribute to the reasons people look forward to gathering together as a church family in the weeks that follow.

One lesson from these approaches is that increasing worship attendance is not always about reaching out to those in the larger community who are not yet connected to a church. Sometimes it is as simple as finding ways to engage current church members. Special efforts to help those already committed to become more faithful in their participation as disciples of Christ is one key to helping the church experience deeper discipleship and more loving fellowship. When people experience their church as a place of vitality and a community that honors the commitment of the young and remembers the contributions and gifts of its older members, people are far more likely to share their excitement about the church with neighbors and friends. This positive interaction about the church is the best evangelism a congregation can find. It suggests that on any given Sunday, the decision to miss church may be a decision to miss the people and practices that are most valuable to our lives.

SUMMER[1]

In most churches, summer is considered a "low time" when worship attendance slips far below what is average at other times of the year. But planning for summer worship with the assumption that there will be fewer people can easily become a self-fulfilling prophecy. More and more, churches are finding that with careful planning, the sharp drop in summer worship attendance can be avoided. And avoiding that big dip in the summer—

- will help keep positive momentum going,

- will reinforce the expectation of regular attendance,

- will create a more welcoming environment for summer visitors,

- will pave the way for a stronger start in the fall, and

- will make a big difference in improving a church's annual worship attendance.

Above all, the congregation will be more likely to have the opportunity to reach more new disciples for Jesus Christ and will help those already within the community of faith to grow in their discipleship.

Churches that take low attendance in the summer as a given tend to reduce their programming and scale back their worship services. In many churches, the summer involves a "change of pace" with adjustments in worship times, the number of services, the type of music, and other variations.

These changes may seem appropriate at first because fewer people may be attending, and clergy and staff will be joining parishioners in taking annual summer vacations. But this approach can inadvertently reinforce a cycle of declining summer attendance because it sends the signal to people that it is not important to come. People start thinking, "We won't really be missing anything if we don't attend church in the summer."

The Tully Principle of "52 Equal Sundays"

This "52 Equal Sundays" concept is from the Reverend Bill Tully, recently retired rector of St. Bartholomew's Episcopal Church on Park Avenue in New York City. When he arrived at the church in 1994, it was reaching only 125 people each Sunday. Tully is credited with turning St. Bart's around. And in the process, he developed several principles for growing churches.

One of them is the concept of "52 Equal Sundays." He contends that it sends the wrong message when you almost close down for some or all of the summer months. "When people come to your church, you want to be doing your best work always. The goal is 52 equal Sundays." The key point is to provide the same high-quality worship experience every Sunday of the year—to have the kind of powerful worship every week that will give the greatest opportunity to reach any person who chooses to worship at your church that day. This does not mean that every element of worship needs to be exactly the same all through the year, but it needs to be of the same high quality.[2]

Why Summer Matters

First, unless your congregation is made up entirely of people who own two homes or who can afford to take three-month vacations every summer, it is a myth that everyone is gone all summer. Many people go on vacation for a week or two, and maybe they take a weekend away here and there over the summer. But that does not add up to everyone being gone all summer. Yet somehow, we tend to slip into that way of thinking.

Second, and perhaps most important, people are more likely to visit churches over the summer. Why? Because individuals and families are more likely to relocate over the summer months and more people are traveling. So you need to ask, "Would someone visiting our church over the summer experience the best of what our church has to offer?"

In fact, summer can be the perfect time to focus especially on attracting newcomers. For example, The Journey Church in New York City has seen growth each summer by using June, July, and August to reach new people through creative outreach that takes advantage of the season. They take advantage of the outdoor lifestyle of the summer by increasing their presence through "servant evangelism" (giving out bottles of water, for example) in the parks or at outdoor events people are attending.[3]

Next, for many people, the slower pace of summer may mean they have more time and energy for church. What is the number one reason people say they cannot engage in church? They are too busy with school, sports, and other activities. The summer may actually be a time when they are freer for and more interested in church activities for adults or for children.

Finally, in many communities and on many campuses today, students return to school in August, not September. So a church that waits until after Labor Day to get back in gear is missing out on this critical time of re-engagement.

What about Vacations?

But what about clergy and staff vacations? They continue as usual. Parts of worship may be done differently and involve different leadership on some Sundays, but you can work to make sure that worshipers will have an experience equally as vital as they would at any other time of the year. It does mean that planning will be required, but all vital worship requires extensive planning.

Summer may be the time for a guest preachers' series to cover the pastor's vacation. It may be a time for a pulpit exchange or a guest choir. But these things can be presented as a positive opportunity, rather than an excuse for worshipers to stay home.

Keep in mind the example of organizations and companies in different sectors whose work is vital 52 weeks of the year—whether that means hospitals or public transportation systems or the police force. They find a way to accommodate vacation schedules and still accomplish their mission. The church's mission in worship 52 weeks a year is equally vital and equally deserving of the effort to keep it "on line" and available year round.

We turn now to various aspects of worship and programming and consider the best ways to keep them strong and vital during the summer.

Worship Schedule and Times

The Lewis Center did an informal survey a few years ago to learn what churches did in the summer in terms of their worship practices. Almost half reported making changes. The most common change—in more than two-thirds of those churches reporting changing their pattern in the summer—was changing the time of one or more of their services. About a third of those reporting a changed pattern reduced the number of services. About 20 percent changed the location of their services.

Does this help or hurt? Ann Michel, associate director of the

Lewis Center, reports an experience from her church. The pattern over many decades had been to have two identical Sunday morning services, at 9:00 a.m. and 11:00 a.m., but only a single service in the summer, at 10:00 a.m. Attendance was always substantially lower in the summer. But everyone said, "Of course it is. It's the summer." Then one year, the formats of the two services had been changed, thus making it more difficult to combine them, so the church stayed with two services all summer. The following year, the church decided to return to the practice of only one summer service, at 10:00 a.m. This allowed an "apples to apples" comparison, week by week across the summer—comparing summer attendance when keeping the normal schedule of two services to that of only one service held at a different time. Week by week, across the summer, the worship attendance was about 15 percent less when there was a single service.

What might cause this decline? Some people might not be open to doing something different. Some become confused. You certainly run the risk of confusing potential visitors or infrequent attendees who may not get the word about a schedule change.

This situation may not be the case in your church. But give careful consideration to the question of changing services and make an honest and fact-based assessment. Do not fall into the trap of assuming that the reason fewer people are coming is because it is summer. It may be because you have "messed with" what they are used to.

Preaching and Sermons

Summer is a time to be especially creative and select topics that will draw persons to worship. For example, one church does a summer sermon series on God at the movies, pulling spiritual themes from the summer's biggest blockbuster films. Another church used the July 4 weekend as the launching point for a

115

series on the faith of the presidents. The key question is what will spark the interest of those in your community. Summer is also a good time to bring in a guest preacher who will draw members and visitors. One church in downtown Washington, DC, for example, has a highly advertised great theologians series in the summer. Several shorter sermon series or stand-alone topics might work better than a longer sermon series in the summer because you do not want to discourage those who cannot attend consistently week after week all summer.

Music

Music is an area where creative planning is needed to maintain high quality, since your music director, choir members, or other musicians may have some time away during the summer. But you want to avoid the situation where your entire music ministry takes a three-month break.

Ask choir members to provide their vacation schedules, if possible, at the beginning of the summer. If you see a week many of the men will be away, consider featuring an all-female group. If many of the women will be gone, feature a barbershop quartet. Plan your music accordingly.[4]

You can also promote the idea of a "summer choir" made up of regular choir members who are present and any other members of the congregation who might like the opportunity to join in when they are available. Select easy-to-sing music. Some churches find it helpful to have choir practice immediately before the service, instead of another day of the week, to make it easier for people to join in.

Summer is also a time to use special music as a way to draw others to worship. Maybe it can be a guest choir or a musical presentation from your Vacation Bible School children. Such special music times become an opportunity to invite people to church.

Sunday School and Children's Programming

Worship attendance can—and probably will—drop off if Sunday school ends for a time in the summer. You will have a drop because families who made an effort to get to church in order to bring their children to Sunday school now do not have that reason to come. Plus, if they do come, there is nothing special for their children.

One solution is to provide year-round Sunday school—or, if that is not possible, to provide alternate programming for children. This needs to be high quality—not just showing a video. In one church, the children all worked on a drama project one year over the summer that culminated in a special worship presentation. Another year, there was a summer emphasis on service for children and families. Each Sunday, there was a special service project for them. One family was asked to take charge of the activity each week so that the responsibility did not fall to the regular Sunday school teachers. In a smaller church, you might offer a one-room-schoolhouse format in the summer.[5]

The idea is to provide a reason for families to want to come to church. We used to assume that parents would bring their children to church. It is now often the case that children bring their parents to church. So if there is something creative and engaging for children, more families will come.

Youth

Summer offers wonderful opportunities to engage youth. Yes, they have other activities and work, but they also have time. It is fine to designate a staff person or volunteer to plan youth programs, but think also of expanded ways in which summer might be a time to integrate youth more substantially in worship and other ministries. Be especially attentive to ways in which youth and adults can serve together. Many youth are good candidates for the new leaders you hope to engage for short-term ministry commitments during the summer. Take youth seriously, and take advantage of the time and desire for service many of them possess.

Many student ministry groups travel to service camps in the summer. They may perform home improvement tasks or build wheelchair ramps for older adults or persons with disabilities. Some travel to urban centers and work in a variety of settings, from meals-on-wheels programs to shelters for homeless persons. In the evening, these middle and high school students typically share in a time of Bible study and reflection on what God has shown them during the day. A special service after they return that is led by the students and incorporates both pictures and stories of their trip, as well as their testimonies, is a fine way to highlight the unique contributions of this group and include their families and friends in worship.

Adult Education and Groups

The same principle applies to adult education and groups. If your regular adult classes and groups do not meet in the summer, it is a good time to offer other possibilities, such as short-term studies and one-time educational events. One church did an adult forum on figures from the Bible. Church members presented one of their own favorite biblical characters. It was launched on the July 4 weekend, and the attendance was still strong because of the effort put into making it something special and inviting new leaders to be engaged. Summer is a great time to try new initiatives and involve new people.

Take Advantage of Seasonal Opportunities

Beyond trying to maintain the basics of high-quality worship and programming over the summer, the season can present unique opportunities for reaching out to particular constituencies and planning special events.

Ask some key questions:

What is going on in the summer? Maybe you do a Vacation Bible School or a family camp or you send out mission teams in the summer. If you have these kinds of activities, they can be the springboard for a special focus in worship.

What is appropriate to the season? There may be special events in the summer that would encourage people to attend church, such as an after-church picnic or ice cream social. Summer might be a time to add an evening service—either on a weeknight or on Sunday night—especially intended for those who are out of town over the weekend. But note that this would be in addition to, not in place of, your Sunday service. You might want to encourage casual dress in the summer if that is not already the pattern at your church. Or you might have events that build upon popular community events and outdoor activities, such as the county fair or the community Fourth of July celebration.

Cautions and Concerns

If your church is firmly in the habit of scaling things back in the summer, there may be resistance when you suggest "raising the bar" in the summertime. It is not going to be the people in the pews enjoying a higher quality of worship who will be complaining. The most grumbling will likely come from those on the church staff or those in leadership roles who have gotten into the habit of thinking they can take it easy in the summer. So it is very important to make the case for why worship matters in the summer, to be sure key leaders are involved, to remind people why what they do matters to God and to others, and to model a positive, can-do attitude.

You may need to start small. If you are in the habit of scaling back worship starting on Memorial Day, wait until the Fourth of July. If you have been changing your worship schedule in June,

July, and August, maybe you can reduce that to only August, or whatever makes the most sense in your setting. This will allow people to see the possibilities and test the impact on attendance. But do not experiment endlessly, or change things back and forth, because that will cause confusion.

Summer Can Be a Time of Creative Outreach and Growth

Summer can be a time for tremendous creativity and growth—if we are willing to make the effort. Summer is one of the best times of the year to reach out to the community around you. People are more likely to be out and about, so you can make connections with people you may never see in another season. It is a fruitful time for creative, community-based outreach events.

In the summer, people are much more open to doing something that does not fit with their normal routine. Because the atmosphere is more casual, it is easier for people to step into leadership with the freedom to do something a little different. So it is an ideal time to get new people involved, whether it is as worship participants, choir members, or group or children's activity leaders.

This gives your regular leaders a break while creating a safe space for new people to step in and try something with a limited time commitment. When you approach summer scheduling in this way, summer can become a training ground for engaging new leaders.

Summer is a time to think "outside the box" both in terms of what you do and who does it. In the first chapter of Genesis, we read how God ordained the seasons, by setting the sun and moon in the sky, to separate day from night, and as a sign of the seasons. The summer is by God's design a season of growth and fruitfulness. Let it be so in the life of your congregation as well.

Special Focus Sundays

One could say that our lives are made up of 365 days each year. But some of those days are far more special than others, and their celebration brings energy and joy. Birthdays, anniversaries, graduations, weddings, and reunions all punctuate our year in marvelous ways. Then there are special celebrations around national holidays. The Christian year also gives us seasons and days of particular celebration and meaning. Much of our worship life is built around those days.

Just as individuals and families have their own distinctive cluster of special days, growing congregations often have special focus days during the year as one means of sustaining and increasing attendance. They are opportunities to reach out to those who have not yet heard the Gospel message and to deepen the discipleship of those who have already committed themselves to Christ.

It is a common practice among many growing churches to have Sundays during the year with a special focus as a way of sustaining energy and attendance and providing opportunities to invite both members and visitors. Several examples featured in our discussion of low times are special focus Sundays. While they can be done throughout the year, of course, low times might be an especially good time for them, particularly during the summer. Summer options might include a recognition of Volunteers in Mission participants, a Sunday to thank first responders or teachers in your community, or a celebration of the students or teachers in your Sunday school, preschool, or daycare. Some have a blessing of the backpacks Sunday as school resumes.

What is a Special Focus Sunday?

A special focus Sunday is an opportunity to reach more members and visitors through a well-prepared and promoted emphasis on a particular cause or constituency. But a word of caution is necessary. Special focus Sundays do not mean turning your worship hour over to a particular group or agenda. This approach would not always lead to a consistently high level of quality in worship. Many pastors have been approached by outside groups who want to advertise their ministry and take an offering for its support. These speakers often take more time than they promise and may come with a message or speaking style that detracts from the vitality of worship. Rather, the idea is to incorporate this focus into your normal worship and to build attendance by encouraging all those connected with the special focus to attend.

What Are the Benefits of a Special Focus Sunday?

Some of the benefits include the following:

- an occasion to invite members and visitors. Inviting people for a special focus is generally much easier than a general invitation.

- an opportunity to reach more and different people

- increased interest from at least some part of the congregation and community

- an opportunity for attention from the media

Where Do We Start?

The first step is to identify the special focus Sundays you already have during the year in addition to Easter and Christmas. Perhaps your church has a homecoming Sunday, a Mother's Day or Father's Day observance, a blessing of the animals, or some other special focus Sunday. You will want to evaluate each one with questions such as the following:

- Is there still energy around this occasion?

- Is the attendance well above our normal attendance?

- Is it still appropriate as a special focus for the congregation?

- Does it reach people beyond our usual attendees?

- Should we continue this? If so, how can we build on it?

What Else Should We Consider?

Once you have identified your current special focus Sundays, you might consider what other options some churches choose for special focus Sundays. These other options may replace or add to what you are now doing.

Back to school: One of the most common special focus Sundays occurs in the fall once school resumes. It is a way to kick off fall worship and programming in a special way. A church with a very strong church school did this through a Sunday school rally day the first Sunday after Labor Day. Others have their special day a few weeks after Labor Day to provide more promotion time. Churches where schools resume well before Labor Day find it important to have a special Sunday associated with the beginning of school, and then they are able to come back with another special time in early fall.

All Saints Sunday: Some churches observe All Saints Sunday in a way that reaches more people and builds deeper relationships. One model is to invite the families of all members who have died in the past year to be present. Their loved ones are remembered by the reading of each name and the sounding of a chime as the congregation celebrates those no longer with them.

Community recognitions: Some churches have Sundays where they celebrate their connections to the community by recognition of an important group, perhaps scouts, police, or firefighters.

Long-time members: As noted earlier, one church found that marking Memorial Day weekend as a time to recognize those who had been members there for forty years or more was a very significant time of worship and celebration.

Confirmation Sunday: Also referenced in the early part of this chapter is how churches that have moved the reception of confirmands from Easter to the Sunday after Easter or Pentecost Sunday often find that this scheduling is better for everyone. They also are often able to reach those who have not been part of the church before. Finding a way to encourage these guests to return should be a part of the planning process for this event.

These are a few examples that can be supplemented out of your experience at your current church and what other churches have found valuable.

What Do We Need to Do?

The first step is to determine what special focus Sundays you already have that should be continued. Then, in light of those, are there additional special focus Sundays that it might be helpful to add in the coming year?

For each of the days, consider these factors:

- purpose

- those you seek to reach

- attendance goal

- careful preparation

- thorough promotion

- planned and executed follow-up

A planning guide is included at the end of this chapter. Careful planning and hard work will reap blessings for the people of your church and community.

PLANNING A SPECIAL FOCUS SUNDAY

After thinking of a special focus Sunday (either existing or new) to emphasize in the coming months, outline your ideas and plans using the categories below.

Name of the special focus Sunday: _____

_____

State the purpose: _____

_____

Whom are you trying to reach? _____

_____

What is your attendance goal? _____

_____

Steps to take in preparing for this special focus in worship:

1. _____

   _____

2. _____

   _____

3. _____

   _____

4. _____

   _____

5. _____

   _____

6. _____

   _____

Steps to take in promoting this special focus Sunday to build attendance with those you seek to reach:

1. _____

2. _____

3. _____

4. _____

5. _____

6. _____

Ways to follow up with those attending on a special focus Sunday. In addition to normal visitor follow-up procedures, are there specific ways to encourage these guests to return, such as invitations to activities, classes, or prayer groups linked to the theme?

1. _____

2. _____

3. _____

4. _____

5. _____

6. _____

THE WONDER OF WORSHIP

Wonder is the most generative experience related to worship. It is a condition that must be present in the life of those gathered in the sanctuary if worship is to take place. Wonder enables people to return to worship week after week without the experience growing dull or obligatory. When persons experience wonder, they will fulfill the commandment to love God with all their *heart, soul, mind, and strength.*

Most people find their wonder about God as the creator and preserver of the universe. This is why people who do not attend church often say that they find God on the hiking trail rather than the sanctuary. They are not simply giving an excuse for why they do not attend a church service. They find God more tangible, even more believable, while standing on a mountain vista or while gazing at a moonlit night sky. Transcendent moments come when we consider ourselves in the context of the stars, the variety of living organisms of the earth, and the seven billion other humans on the planet. We see the enormity of God's creativity and power while, at the same time, grasping our finitude. It is the opposite of the oversized ego that characterizes the hubris so often demonstrated by humanity. In a state of wonder, we stand in an open posture of praise. Perhaps that is the reason that Jesus encouraged his disciples to have the faith of a child. Children seem predisposed toward wonder.

Tom was at a church gathering that began with an hour of business. He was sitting on the front pew next to a young mother with two children, a girl about ten and a boy, five. The children were well behaved, but Tom knew that they were bored, bored, bored. They had scraps of paper and a pencil. They did some drawing and played tic-tac-toe. Tom was watching this because he was also a bit bored himself. He knew that he would be presenting for about an hour after the business was concluded and thought, "If they aren't bored by now, they surely will be soon."

During a short break, Tom reached into his briefcase and handed the mom a pad of paper, saying, "Let your kids use this if they get fidgety; ask them to draw me some pictures." She thanked Tom and tore some paper off for each of the children. An hour later, Tom was finished and was greeting a short line of people. He noticed the five-year-old boy at the end of the line. The boy was holding two rolled-up sheets of paper.

The boy said, "I have something for you."

"What is it?" Tom asked.

He did not miss a beat. With a very serious tone, he said, "I made you something. Do you have any tape at your house?"

"Yes, I do," Tom replied.

The boy held up together the two sheets of rolled-up paper, end-to-end. "When you get home, get some tape. Put these together like this. Then tape them together. Do you know what that is?"

Tom thought for a minute and recalled what it was like to be a boy and said, "Maybe a sword."

The child's eyes grew big. "That's right! But not just any sword. It is one of those double light sabers. You hold it right on the tape, and it goes both ways."

Tom held the two pieces of paper together with his hand in the center, turning them left and right. "Do you mean like this?"

The boy said, "Yes!"

Tom said slowly, "THAT IS AWESOME!"

The boy said, "I KNOW!"

Tom could tell by the look on the child's face that this five-year-old was grateful that there was finally someone who could see how great this was.

The boy had wonder all over his face.

What if God is like a five-year-old waiting to see if we will experience a sense of wonder at what God has created? What if God is waiting to see if those beings with the capacity to appreciate the intricacies and craftsmanship of the universe will join in the joy of its Creator?

This is the first wonder of worship. The author of Psalm 19 must have held this same look of wonder when writing:

> The heavens declare the glory of God;
> the skies proclaim the work of his hands. (Psalm 19:1)

The psalmist tells us that even the creation itself reflects the beauty of God's imprint. Looking around the world, the writer is amazed at what God has created. The imagination and appreciation of the psalmist, who has the ability to look at everything from the blue of the sky to the surprise of a shooting star and feel a bit of amazement at what God has made, is a prerequisite for worship and thanksgiving.

Here is where wonder turns to worship: the author connects the order of the universe to the nature of our Creator:

> In the heavens he has pitched a tent for the sun,
> which is like a bridegroom coming out of his chamber,
> like a champion rejoicing to run his course.
> It rises at one end of the heavens
> and makes its circuit to the other;
> nothing is deprived of its warmth. (Psalm 19:4b–6)

The psalmist is saying that just as the sun reaches out and brings light and warmth to every point on the globe and nothing stays in the shadows, even if it wanted to, so does the love of God move to the ends of the world, falling on us all. Imagine how such a person enters a sanctuary. There would be an anticipation and excitement that would allow true worship.

Reading just six verses of this psalm, one has to wonder at the psalmist's wonder, be in awe of the awe expressed, and marvel at the marvel uttered.

Worship is the way we keep our eyes and ears open to the wonders of God. We make discoveries about the nature of God that would have otherwise remained unseen. In worship we bring our thanksgiving and praise with us to share with our God. It has the effect of right-sizing our lives before God. Suddenly God is so big, and we are so small.

That humility enables us to turn to God for guidance and instruction. If God is so great as to create a sun that millions of miles away in space is bringing light and warmth, then maybe, just maybe, God has wisdom for our lives that would be helpful. In offering our praise and thanksgiving to God, we gain humility that opens our lives to what God is offering to us.

There is another aspect to wonder in worship that is equally important. It is the wonder of considering how, after thousands of years of existence, humanity has progressed so little on its own. While our technology has grown remarkably, the essential human condition is largely unchanged since the time of our first ancestors. The basic problems of humanity are still the same, from our personal struggles with a variety of moral issues from lying to addiction, to our limited ability to maintain healthy interpersonal relationships such as marriage, to our inability to overcome the basic societal ills of poverty, war, racism, violence, and ignorance. Whether thinking of our personal lives, our society of origin, or other countries of earth, it is a wonder that we are here at all. This is a wonder at human sin, pride, arrogance, and folly. Like our wonder at God, this recognition tends to make us feel small as well. The posture is closed, as one kneeling in repentance.

With such humility, we become teachable. God wants to give us something to bless us in the midst of hardship, and times of corporate and private worship tend to be the place where that happens. What God wants to give us is a good life. God wants to give us a life where we will have a sense of personal integrity and be proud of the way we live and behave. God wants to give us good relationships with people at home and in our work. God wants to give us a life that people will remember with joy and respect because we have been such a blessing to others.

There is a biblical word for the wisdom that our God desires to impart. The word is Torah. Torah refers to the first five books of the Hebrew Bible. But it is more. Jewish tradition describes these books as containers of the ethical wisdom of God for a life of righteousness. This is a life the way God would have it lived. Over time, as we relate to God humbly and hear the scripture or sermons that God might use to speak to us, we become transformed by God's instruction. God uses worship to speak truth into our lives and point us to the goodness of God's love and God's way. Listen to how the author puts it in Psalm 19:7–8 (NRSV):

> The law of the LORD is perfect,
> reviving the soul;
> the decrees of the LORD are sure,
> making wise the simple;
> the precepts of the LORD are right,
> rejoicing the heart;
> the commandment of the LORD is clear,
> enlightening the eyes.

Here the psalmist talks about the wonder of God's Torah and believes that we need these truths because of the pervasive condition of sin in our lives. The author is telling us that the wisdom of God can revive, or bring new life, to our existence that will lead us to have the experience of joy:

the fear of the LORD is pure,
enduring forever;
the ordinances of the LORD are true
and righteous altogether.
More to be desired are they than gold,
even much fine gold;
sweeter also than honey,
and drippings of the honeycomb.
Moreover by them is your servant warned;
in keeping them there is great reward.
But who can detect their errors?
Clear me from hidden faults. (Psalm 19:9–12, NRSV)

When we fail to worship, either through absence or a lack of true participation when we are present, God cannot speak to us about a life that would be a better alternative to the one we are living. Without the presence of God in our lives, we are left to our own undetected errors and hidden faults. We are truly helpless to find a path to transformation. Many people live unconsidered lives, free of the call and influence of God's wisdom and the gateway of confession that leads to applying such wisdom.

In his book *Hiking Through: One Man's Journey to Peace and Freedom on the Appalachian Trail,* Paul Stutzman shares his account of hiking the length of the Appalachian Trail after the death of his wife. He considered himself a Christian, but his wife's death had caused him to grow distant from God and complacent about his faith. As Stutzman begins the hike, he has two prayers: he wants a sense of comfort from his loss, and he desires a sense that God is real and God cares. He wants to regain his sense of wonder about God. He finds this about a month into his adventure as he gains a deeper awareness of the beauty of nature. He is in awe at what God has done in creation.

One day on the trail, he approaches a young man hiking in front of him. Stutzman speaks to the young man, but the other hiker does not respond. Stutzman noticed that this young man had earphones on and was listening to music. Stutzman walked past him and waved. There was still no response.

A short time later, Stutzman began to hear the sound of thunder and realized a storm was coming. He found shelter on the porch of a small church building just a short distance from the trail. The rain started pouring down. A short time later, Stutzman noticed the young man still hiking on the trail, getting drenched. The young man did not see the shelter of the church, so Stutzman called out to him. Unfortunately, the young man still had headphones on and did not hear the shouts. Stutzman continued to yell, but to no avail.

That evening, after he finished the day's hike, Stutzman got into a sleeping bag in his tent. He thanked God for the beauty of creation and prayed a prayer of gratitude for his heightened awareness of God's presence in his life. Stutzman said that in that moment of private worship, the Spirit spoke to his mind, reminding him of the young man wearing the headphones, pointing out that most people live their whole lives in a similarly oblivious way. God is all around, God is speaking, sometimes even calling out in the midst of a storm, but we do not notice and do not hear because we are distracted, or choosing to listen to other things.[1]

We would not be drenched so often in life if we sought the instruction of our God in worship. It is amazing that God loves us so much that Christ has come to teach us how to live, how to treat others, how to serve, and how to bring our own beauty to the world. Not only that, but the Holy Spirit comes to remind us of everything Christ has taught us so that these lessons can inform our lives each day. But we must be humble enough to hear the message and open enough to take it in. Worship brings us to a teachable size by diminishing our ego and transforming the mind that believes it already knows what it needs to know.

Worship enables us to think about our lives in the light of God's love and holiness. During a sermon series entitled "Stung by the Tongue" at the church Tom serves, the congregation read scripture, talked, and prayed about what it meant to be careful with words. After three weeks, a church member came to Tom and said, "What is happening on Sunday is changing how my family talks and treats each other through the week. You know, it's been powerful to see what is happening."

On a different Sunday, the choir's anthem was called "The Offering." Tom watched a woman sitting in a pew as the choir sang. Her eyes were closed, but as that music washed over her, it appeared that she was experiencing something divine. She came out of the service with a joy that was evident to all who interacted with her.

Several years ago, during a sermon, Tom shared an account of a woman in Nicaragua who walked to town each day, begging for food for children in her orphanage. She and the children subsisted on chicken skins given to her by a local poultry processing plant and whatever vegetables she could buy with the money given to her. A member of the church said that after Tom gave the benediction, he felt the hand of God pushing him back down in his seat. He felt God say, "You just sit here and think about that woman." And so he and his wife sat in the sanctuary for thirty minutes, talking and praying about the woman who ran the orphanage.

The Spirit so convicted this couple that they invaded their child's college fund and gave an anonymous offering the congregation matched that bought a year's worth of meals for the children of the orphanage. People from the church went there to serve with her. She never begged again.

These are the kinds of things that happen routinely when

136

people worship. So many other stories could be told as well of those who forgave others who had hurt them, or the person who decided not to consider ending her life, or the man whose life was changed because God asked him to teach third grade Sunday school, all right in the middle of worship.

Worship is powerful. It changes lives. If you want to do something to increase the joy of God and bless others, then it will be important to figure out how to make worship more real, more communal, more personal, and more inclusive. When they gather in their wonder of God and the recognition that what God has to offer is fundamentally better than what they have, lives will transform. In ways small and large, worship is a key to the transformation of the world.

CONCLUSION

IF CHURCHES CAN CHANGE, THEY CAN GROW

Yes, the world has changed, and not in ways that make it easier for churches. But there is good news. The subtitle of a major research report on growing churches is "If churches can change, they can grow."[1]

It is good when churches want to reach new disciples, but desire alone is not enough. Some changes must take place. Everything does not have to change, but everything cannot stay the same, either. This is particularly true in seeking to reach people different from yourselves.

At a minimum, churches need to assess carefully their worship offerings to make sure that the number of services, times of services, and types of worship fit your desire to help current members grow and to reach new disciples. The reality for growing churches is that countless changes are occurring regularly in response to ongoing review and feedback. Some of the changes are bold and evident to everyone, while most are far more subtle and less obvious.

This is where churches face a dilemma. Change usually leads to conflict, but change is required to make progress. Drawing upon research with congregations over five years, David Brubaker found that the two issues most likely to cause conflict are a

139

change in the governance system and a change in worship. A church making one of these changes is 3.3 times more likely to experience major conflict than churches not making the change. If a church takes on both of these in the same year, the church is seven times more likely to have conflict. Churches that are growing rapidly are more likely to have conflict than are stable churches, but the churches with the highest rates of conflict are those declining rapidly.

These statistics remain the same across various sizes of churches. Brubaker captures the tension when he says that congregations "that adapt their worship services—especially by adding a new worship service—are indeed at a higher risk of conflict. But congregations that fail to adapt to a changing environment may be at much greater risk."[2]

So if change is essential for progress, how can change be handled in such a way as to minimize destructive conflict that often results in members leaving and leaders having to be replaced? Brubaker found it of particular interest that one major change is less likely to cause conflict: building projects. While there are exceptions, for the most part churches have learned well over the years some basic steps to take in embarking on a building project—steps that help people get on board with the change. When considering the care with which such a project is generally begun—listening sessions, information sharing, timelines, question sessions, and so on—one can immediately see how casually we often undertake other major efforts in the church, including changes in worship.

Building programs require substantial congregational support to succeed. That is why such projects are approached with great care and planning. New worship undertakings require just as much understanding and support. So think of a new worship initiative as if it were a new building project and then develop similar steps to build understanding and support. Brubaker finds two concepts from Paul in 1 Corinthians that we all might use

140

in implementing change: orderliness and love. Working carefully on the plan with a great deal of openness and transparency, along with a never-failing attitude of love for all involved, just might permit change that builds up the body of Christ.[3]

FIELDS RIPE UNTO HARVEST

A recent Pew Research Center report[4] on changes in religious affiliation in the United States received major attention among both secular and religious media. A troubling finding is that one in five adults claims no religious affiliation. And among adults under age thirty, one in three claims no religious affiliation. These figures continue a trend over recent years, but the pace of growth in the "nones," as they are called, is quite disturbing, even though some of that growth may be attributed to people becoming more comfortable reporting no affiliation. Such cultural trends only exacerbate the church's continuing struggles with reaching more people, particularly younger and more diverse people.

But the survey also makes clear that most of the "nones" have not given up on the spiritual quest. Two-thirds believe in God, and a quarter pray every day. People are still interested in their relationship with God, the purpose of life, and release from all that enslaves the human spirit today. They are just not interested in what institutional church leaders are offering.

As we said at the beginning, it may seem strange to speak of opportunities for churches when there are so many discouraging trends for many churches. Circumstances may not be particularly promising, but the boundless love and grace of God revealed in Jesus Christ is sufficient enough that we are bold in speaking in the title of this book of "overflow." Such an abundant harvest comes not from our ingenuity but from God's power. We must always be careful to remember that while we may do the planting and watering, the growth always comes from God (1 Corinthians 3:6).

There are many people in all our communities who may have given up on church but not on God. God is alive. God is able. The human need for God has not changed. Indeed, souls continue to be restless until they find their rest in God.

The question for us is "Are we representing the God we know in Jesus Christ in ways so that all know that our hope for every person in our community is the same as that of Jesus, that all 'may have life, and have it abundantly'?" (John 10:10b, NRSV).

We pray that you will treat all of this new learning with much prayer and discernment and with hearts and minds open to "the new thing" God may be trying to do in your midst. May God give you clues about making your church and your worship more responsive to the yearnings of current members and those who come to your church seeking new life in Christ.

NOTES

Introduction

1. Tom Berlin and Lovett H. Weems, Jr., *Bearing Fruit: Ministry with Real Results* (Nashville: Abingdon Press, 2011), chapter 3.

2. For a discussion of this worship downturn and possible reasons, see Lovett H. Weems, Jr., "No Shows," *Christian Century*, October 5, 2010, 10–11.

3. We are grateful to David McAllister-Wilson, president of Wesley Theological Seminary in Washington, DC, for these insights.

3. Pay Attention to Worship Services

1. Nelson Searcy, *The Worship Planning Seminar* (CD; Church Leader Insights, 2008). A superb book on worship planning based on this seminar is Nelson Searcy and Jason Hatley, *Engage: A Guide to Creating Life-Transforming Worship Services* (Grand Rapids: Baker Books, 2011).

2. An essential resource for pastors in developing their preaching plans is Adam Hamilton, *Unleashing the Word: Preaching with Relevance, Purpose, and Passion* (Nashville: Abingdon Press, 2003). Hamilton outlines five areas of preaching that the pastor should address during the course of a year: evangelism, discipleship, pastoral care, equipping and sending, and institutional development.

3. Searcy, *Engage*, 168.

4. Ibid., 39.

4. Pay Attention to Attendance Seasons and Patterns

1. For more information on the Congregational Attendance Profile, go to http://www.churchleadership.com/CAP/default.asp.

5. Big Days

1. To read about one church's experience with such services, see Jessica Anschutz, "Travelers' Christmas Eve Service," *Leading Ideas*, online newsletter of the Lewis Center for Church Leadership, October 27, 2010, accessed June 2, 2013, http://www.churchleadership.com/leadingideas/leaddocs/2010/101027_article.html.

7. Low Times

1. Ann A. Michel, associate director of the Lewis Center for Church Leadership, contributed significantly to this section.

2. Lovett H. Weems, Jr., "The Tully Principle of 52 Equal Sundays," *Leading Ideas,* online newsletter of the Lewis Center for Church Leadership, April 7, 2011, accessed June 20, 2013, http://www.churchleadership.com/leadingideas/leaddocs/2007/070411_article.html.

3. Nelson Searcy, *Maximizing Summer: A Special Report by Nelson Searcy* (New York: Church Leader Insights, 2008).

4. "Stop Singing the Summer Attendance Blues," United Methodist Communications, accessed June 20, 2013, http://www.umcom.org/site/apps/nlnet/content3.aspx?c=mrLZJ9PFKmG&b=6084927&ct=10856675.

5. For more on the one-room Sunday school format, see Lewis A. Parks, "The One Room (Church) School House," *Leading Ideas,* online newsletter of the Lewis Center for Church Leadership, October 10, 2012, accessed June 1, 2013, http://www.churchleadership.com/leadingideas/leaddocs/2012/121010_article2.html.

8. The Wonder of Worship

1. Paul Stutzman, Hiking Through: One Man's Journey to Peace and Freedom on the Appalachian Trail (Grand Rapids: Revell, 2012), 126–28.

Conclusion

1. C. Kirk Hadaway, "FACTS on Growth 2010," *Faith Communities Today,* December 19, 2011, accessed June 2, 2013, http://faithcommunitiestoday.org/facts-growth-2010.

2. David R. Brubaker, "The Promise and Peril of Conflict," *Leading Ideas,* online newsletter of the Lewis Center for Church Leadership, August 4, 2010, accessed June 20, 2013, http://www.churchleadership.com/leadingideas/leaddocs/2010/100804_article.html. For a more expansive treatment of the topic by the author, see David R. Brubaker, *Promise and Peril: Understanding and Managing Change and Conflict in Congregations* (Herndon, VA: Alban Institute, 2009).

3. Ibid.

4. "'Nones' on the Rise: One-in-Five Adults Have No Religious Affiliation," *The Pew Forum on Religion & Public Life,* October 9, 2012, accessed June 2, 2013, http://www.pewforum.org/Unaffiliated/nones-on-the-rise.aspx.